FLYOVER LIVES

Also by Diane Johnson

Lulu in Marrakech

Into a Paris Quartier:
Reine Margot's Chapel and Other Haunts of St.-Germain

L'Affaire

Le Mariage

Le Divorce

Natural Opium: Some Travel Takes

Health and Happiness

Persian Nights

Dashiell Hammett: A Life

Terrorists and Novelists: Essays

Lying Low

The Shadow Knows

Burning

Loving Hands at Home

Fair Game

Diane Johnson

FLYOVER LIVES

A Memoir

VIKING

VIKING

Published by the Penguin Group

Penguin Group (USA) LLC

375 Hudson Street

New York, New York 10014

USA | Canada | UK | Ireland | Australia | New Zealand | India | South Africa | China

penguin.com

A Penguin Random House Company

First published by Viking Penguin, a member of Penguin Group (USA) LLC, 2014

Portions of this book appeared in different form as "The Generals" in *National Post*
(Toronto), "The Writing Life" in *The Washington Post*, "Stanley Kubrick: 1928–1999" in
The New York Review of Books, and "A Passion for Cars—Just Don't Make Her Drive
Them" in *The New York Times*.

Photograph credits

Pages ix, 123, 140: © Lucy Gray 2013

Page 179: Münchner Stadtmuseum, Sammlung Fotografie, Archiv Landshoff

Other photographs courtesy of the author

LIBRARY OF CONGRESS CATALOGING,IN,PUBLICATION DATA

Johnson, Diane, 1934–

Flyover lives : a memoir / Diane Johnson.

pages cm

ISBN 978,0,670,01640,2

1. Johnson, Diane, 1934– —Family.   2. Moline (Ill.)—Biography.
3. Pioneers—Middle West—Biography.   4. Home—Middle West.   5. Middle
West—Biography.   6. Middle West—Social life and customs.   7. Novelists,
American—Biography.   I. Title.

PS3560.O3746Z46 2014

813'.54—dc23

[B]   2013036808

Printed in the United States of America

1 3 5 7 9 10 8 6 4 2

Set in Pastonchi MT Std

Designed by Francesca Belanger

To my husband, John,
to James, Douglas, Kevin, Darcy, Liz, Amanda, and Simon,
and in loving memory of all the ghosts in this book

Portrait of Catharine A. Martin

Chenoa, Illinois, 1876

Knowing how little time (during youth and middle life when people are busy with the cares of life and raising a family) they have to think of their forefathers or to tell their children, I, in my old age will write what I know of my dear husband's family and of my own. And hope no one will destroy or throw away this Book, for I hope some of my grandchildren or grandchildren's children will think enough of their parentage to read what their old grandmother writes when she is . . . 76 years old, and probably will be laid in the dust long before this is looked at.

—Catharine A. Martin

CONTENTS

IV. Modern Days

FOREWORD

I had always wondered how the first settlers in Illinois, in the eighteenth century and the beginning of the nineteenth, survived the ruthless climate and isolation, how they managed to clear the tough woodlands to make their farms, how they taught their kids something about Shakespeare and Mozart, and eventually pitched in for a war like the Civil War though they'd barely seen a black person or encountered a slave. No one writes much about the center part of our country, sometimes called the Flyover, or about the modest pioneers who cleared and peopled this region. Yet their midwestern stories tell us a lot about American history. Migration patterns, wars, the larger movements, are after all made up of individual human beings experiencing and sometimes recording their lives.

Now that circumstance has taken me to live abroad much of the time, or "overseas," as I've learned to say for its hardship military ring, I have wondered more than ever about how the first travelers managed to keep with them some of the qualities of sweetness, stolidity, and common sense they've become reputed for—qualities that are hard to see now in certain politicians who speak for this region.

I became especially interested in some testimonies by long-departed great-grandmothers, simple stories but all the rarer because the lives of prairie women have usually been lost. Perhaps prairie women at the end of the eighteenth century didn't have the leisure to pick up their pens, or maybe they didn't think their lives were of interest. I came to think of the people whose stories I finally uncovered as kin to the Indian ghosts that so fascinated me as a child: wispy but material, brought forth from the dust of old attic trunks, in the voices of unsung and unknown people speaking out now and then about their lives two hundred years ago, people whose thoughts and ways somehow account for much about this country, at least in the flat region of cornfields and bonfires along what used to be called the Illinois Bottom—sometimes French Bottom—or, back in the seventeenth century when people began to move that way, "Louisiane." A millennium before that, in lower Illinois, there was a city of native peoples called Cahokia that was bigger than the London of the time, and now is only a series of excavated mounds.

Maybe, as at the beginning of a Russian novel, I should list the names of some of the people who have spoken out from their jottings and letters on their way to Illinois. The earliest was a Frenchman, René Cossé, who left France in 1711; then his grand, son, a judge in Vermont, Ambrose Cossitt, who was born in 1749 and lived through the Revolutionary War. Ambrose's daughter Anne, born in 1779, left an account of giving birth in an icy cabin up on the border with Canada—and of her religious obses, sions during the Second Great Awakening of fervid piety that swept America at the beginning of the nineteenth century. Her husband, John Perkins, tells about seeing angels and devils—those iconic New England figures that did not seem to follow people to Illinois (though my mother's hometown of Watseka was noted for having a well, documented case of possession, when Lu, rancy Vennum was inhabited by the ghost of Mary Roff).

I'm afraid I found a couple of unreliable characters: Dr. Eleazer Martin and Dr. Charles Stewart Elder both strike me in their letters as a little dodgy in matters of the heart. But we can't choose our relatives, or which of them we take after; we can only try to capture a few traces of them. As Tolstoy tells us, individual stories are what add up to "history." Catharine Martin left a longer memoir of her life with her abolitionist husband, Eleazer, in the newly settled territories of Ohio and Illinois, where they went as newlyweds in 1826. Their son-in-law Charles Elder writes from his encampment during the Civil War. Dolph Lain (my brother's and my father) wrote down his memories of life on an Iowa farm at the end of the nineteenth century, and about going off to the First World War in the early twentieth.

My aunts Martha, Henrietta, and Grace conserved manuscripts and letters that their forebears in the little town of Watseka had been saving since the end of the eighteenth century. One of these is a typescript of an 1879 memoir transcribed by an unknown hand from handwritten pages. Some pages are missing, and I'm not sure where the handwritten manuscript is; cousins are scattered, and all my aunts are dead. Someone who must be a sort of cousin (her name is Susan Lindsay Church) posted a bit of it on a genealogy Web site recently that differs from my longer manuscript. Maybe she has the handwritten manuscript—I wrote to her, but the e-mail came back.

It's certain that its author was my (and maybe the unknown Susan's) great-great-grandmother Catharine Martin (born 1800), who was living in Chenoa, Illinois, when she wrote a hundred pages in 1876, the centenary of the nation, looking back to her own girlhood, telling some stories that give us a glimpse of what a young woman's life was like in the 1820s, newly arrived in the strange new territory. This would have been nearly the same time that in England, Jane Austen was writing her stories about similar young women in a much different, more settled world, and Napoleon had recently sold us Louisiana. My brother, Mike Lain, turned out to have a packet of letters sent to him by Aunt Martha Silliman, a trove of documents and deeds, the earliest of which is from 1796. She must have felt him to be the more reliable of the two Lain kids, Mike and me.

The lives of all these departed people were mostly unremarkable, mostly plain, their cares and anxieties of little interest to anyone but themselves. Other people's aunts and grandfathers have doubtless also left drawers full of things just as revealing of the faded other days, from other attics—mild-mannered testimonies from folks whose voices have long been abashed into silence, aware, perhaps, of their eclipse by more vibrant and clamorous newcomers.

In the interest of completeness I have added some contemporary stories, especially my own story of leaving and going back to have another look at the scenes I had not always remembered exactly. Some of what follows I have written about already—about my yellow Morgan car, for example, and about our summer house, and about becoming a writer, and have borrowed back some of my own words from the *New York Times*, *New York Review of Books*, and *Washington Post*.

I

IN FRANCE

1

A Weekend with Generals

This book of histories about small-town people in the Midwest, including me, begins not in Illinois, where much of it takes place, but in France a few years ago, at a house party in Provence, with something a French friend said about Americans—something I acknowledged to be true and felt sorry about: that we Americans are naïve and indifferent to history. Certainly I was.

The discussion began with her saying, "It's funny the way all Americans believe they are descended from royalty."

We—my husband, John, and I—denied this with some indignation. We were visiting the French friend, Simone Ward, and her American husband, Stuart, a retired army colonel, whom we'd met a few years before on the ski slopes of Courchevel; they ordinarily lived in Virginia, and we saw one another only when we were all in France because our American lives were geographically too far apart. The winter before we had discussed a summer plan: we would be traveling to Italy in August, and Simone and Stuart had invited us to stay a day or two on our way.

Together with American friends of theirs, they were renting a beautiful, big house from a cousin of Simone's—an expensive house, but they were dividing the rent among four couples. We had been interested when Simone told us who these other tenants were—retired military men, old classmates or companions-in-arms of her husband, Stuart. So that's how we had found ourselves surprisingly flung among a gaggle of American army generals in the south of France.

It isn't every day you meet generals—after all, they inhabit another world, inside their bases or stationed overseas. Our own stations in life (doctor, writer) had not brought us into contact with many generals, and never in their military capacity, though we had known a few in the social world: There was Davis B., the husband of my friend Marjorie, whom we met during his retirement, when he opened an antiques business. And my old friend C. is the daughter of a Marine Corps general—an old, senile gentleman when I last saw him, though in his vigorous younger days a fierce Korean War leader.

I also had some childhood memories, on account of having grown up near a minor army post, the Rock Island Arsenal, on a clump of land right in the middle of the Mississippi River, the site of the golf course where my parents played (and an emplacement of slot machines, which were illegal on either shore of the river, that is, in both Illinois and Iowa), an armory, a museum, and neat lines of the graves of Confederate men imprisoned here by the Union army during the Civil War.

John and I live in France now a lot of the time, in Paris, along with thousands of other Americans. He is a professor of medicine with a role in the control of worldwide tuberculosis and other lung diseases, in an organization whose seat is in Paris. Of course we're delighted to live in a pleasant place like Paris, but explaining why you live abroad is always tricky. The one thing you, we, Americans, are not allowed to say is that there is somewhere better than America to live. This is an unspeakable apostasy, even though anyone who has lived in one of the better places knows it's true.

OPPOSITE: *Our hardship post in Paris*

I'm not speaking of morally better, not speaking about virtue, but about livability in the sense that American magazines track the best places, from the points of view of public transport, crime, museums and hospitals and schools and so on. We mustn't say it, but I have noticed that more and more Americans like us are living Elsewhere if they have a good excuse, and this was something inconceivable only a few years ago. Then, you got hardship pay for living Elsewhere.

In my case, living abroad was by accident, John's job. Yet I became aware that he and I were inadvertently part of a historical trend: Americans didn't stop moving once they got to the West Coast, but have moved on, sometimes up to Alaska, sometimes back to roots in the Old World, recapturing the vanished days. More than fifty thousand Americans live in Paris alone.

We'd arrived in Saint-Pantaléon in September. We were in the south of France—was this called the Lot? The Luberon? The region everyone was said to love that to us looked too much like California to be exotic. Even the fire-blighted fields were familiar.

The driveway was long, lined with stiff narrow trees like the Corot painting I remembered on the cover of my second-grade reader. With Venus de Milo on the crayon box, our distant European connections were always before American children, no invocations of Mexico or Cairo back then, except on the packages of Camel cigarettes our mothers smoked.

At the end of the driveway was a gravel turnaround, and beyond that, open gates into a courtyard. At the opposite side of the courtyard, a large house, in what in California we would call the Spanish style, with a tile roof and a vine-covered stucco wall. Several cars were parked at the edges of the turnaround, and a man

stood at the gate, hands in his pockets, smiling at us in a welcoming way, then strolling toward us. It was easy to guess he was one
of the generals Simone and Stuart were sharing the house with.
He was not wearing a uniform, but his close haircut, the compact
fitness of his erect though rather short figure, and the starched
perfection of his shirt, as if he traveled with a batman, revealed
his identity all the same.

"You must be Simone's visitors," he said to us, opening the car
door for me. "Bill Baum." His charm was palpable even in these
few words, a handsome, smiling man whose air of authority left
no doubt that I would be getting out of the car as his gesture required.

We introduced ourselves to General Baum, and embraced Simone, who came flying out of the house. The two men carried into
the kitchen two cases of wine we had brought, and I followed with
a flat of vegetables from a roadside stand that had remained somehow unburned in a swath of singed shrubbery. In the kitchen we
met Mrs. Baum, Cynthia, wearing a scarf over her hair, cooking
something that smelled delicious. She waved her wooden spoon at
us with a conspiratorial, welcoming grin, the complicity and socia-
bility of cooks. The aroma of beef and carrots proclaimed some
sort of Provençale triumph for dinner. The impression of complete
domestic perfection was heightened by meeting Sally Rolfe, the
other general's wife, coming in from the market with her arms full
of gladioli and daylilies.

Both of these women were beautiful, I noted, still beautiful
women in their sixties, slender and straight, each with a varia-
tion of blond hair shading to decorous gray. Obviously they had
been assets to their husbands; perhaps it's indispensable, for becoming a general, to have a beautiful wife. Their slenderness

bespoke military self-discipline; both Sally Rolfe and Cynthia
Baum had the figures of girls.

Our friend Simone's husband, Stuart Ward, was retired with
the rank of colonel because of illness before he could go any
higher, a lymphoma that he had since been cured of; but because
he was charming and clever, he and Simone had remained friendly
with all the people they had started out with when the men were
lieutenants at West Point, or captains together in France in the
Second World War, or perhaps Stuart had served under them, for
they were older than he. Also, Simone and Stuart were known by
others to have some money, and some property, and some beautiful furniture from Simone's side of the family—things to sustain
them at the social level their eventual rank would have predicted,
but for the illness, which could happen to anyone.

Simone and Stuart had borne with dignity the disappointment of Stuart's career, perhaps didn't even feel it, for it was fate
that had dealt it to them, and fate sometimes inflicts a merciful
freedom from self-blame along with its blows. They didn't have
to bear the harder sting of Stuart's having made some personal
error or having a defect of character.

We were led out onto the porches, where the rest of the party
was lying by the pool. Out of earshot, Simone rolled her eyes
and said to us in a low voice, "Thank God you're here. Diver-
sion, dilution." Only then did we notice that she seemed agitated
and tense. Simone is a tall, elegant woman but now with this hint
of distress. She smiled enormously at her friends, but we sensed
a strain at the edge of her teeth, perhaps the normal strain of
anyone who has eight houseguests.

The Lees rose to say hello—tan and lean people a little younger than the others: Lynne and Willard. Willard Lee, like our host, Stuart Ward, was a colonel, or, one should say, only a colonel. Poor Stuart, reddened in the sun, looked wan—he had slowed since we last saw him, and perhaps it was his health that was mak‚ ing Simone tense, or the reminder that if it hadn't been for his health he too would be a general.

I have changed the names of these military people. What if someone reads this whose son had served with them, or who had himself served under them, looked up to and been led by them? People believe in generals, after all. Military figures like Lord Nelson and the Duke of Wellington, or George Washington and Ike, were fathers to their men.

We were installed in pretty rooms in the guesthouse on the other side of the pool. The place looked like nothing so much as the Hotel Bel Air, and I had to remind myself that things in California are often modeled after Provence, not the other way round. We unpacked only a little, as our stay would be short. "It looks like Willard Lee is wearing tennis shorts," John said de‚ lightedly, for he is like a hunter, predatory about possible tennis players, elated to spot one. We expected a pleasant day.

Almost immediately, John was taken off to play singles with Willard Lee, and I sat down with the ladies by the pool. I was some‚ thing of a curiosity—they did not know any writers of fiction, and I became aware that Simone had probably exalted my accomplish‚ ments beyond what they deserved. "It's just incredibly interesting," said Sally Rolfe. "Wherever do you get your ideas from?" She had a Southern accent, one of the Carolinas. So did the other general's wife, Mrs. Baum (Cynthia). The aroma of Cynthia's stew trailed

into the garden, seductive and deep in the hot afternoon. Exhaled
phrases of satisfaction: dinner would be early, and early to bed—
this was the simple, healthy life, how they all would have liked to
live in France, as well as in America, God bless it.

I had to answer any number of questions—whether I use a
pen or pencil or computer, and how long it takes to write a novel.
Despite myself, despite the banality of the questions and the
dozens of times I have answered them, I began to feel fascinating. I saw it was the arts of Mrs. Baum and Mrs. Rolfe that con-
ferred this feeling. Like geishas they worked me, John too, when
he got back from tennis, asking him about the health of the
world and his role in it. Only Lynne Lee (husband just a colonel) betrayed a little prickle of competitive edge when it came to
my writing. "Are you published?" she would say, or "Are your
books for adults?" It was the dark side of military strategy I was
seeing. Cynthia Baum and Sally Rolfe had excelled at concealing
what Lynne Lee more clumsily revealed, the vigilant combative-
ness, the alert defense; their smooth tactical tact disguising a
war machine directed at victory for their husbands.

I had two Siamese cats once who worked in a pair, attacking
marauders. Together they jumped, hissing and screaming, onto
the back of a puppy we brought home. Years before, they had
jumped onto the naked back of a lover (it was John, but they
didn't know him then), mistaking his embrace for aggression. I
thought of those cats because one of them was named Cynthia.
These ladies did not claw the handsome John's back when he
and Willard came in from their tennis (Willard having won);
they purred delightfully at him.

Our friend Simone busied herself carrying trays of drinks in
and out, stringing the beans, folding the serviettes from the

dryer. There was something taciturn and self-sacrificing in her manner, like Martha to the brace of brilliant Marys. Even Cynthia Baum, charged with the dinner—they were taking turns cooking—went at it in the manner of the sprightlier biblical figure, while our poor friend Simone, usually animated, bridge playing, chattering, and fully armed, was now preoccupied, even depressed. I thought she was perhaps worried about Stuart's health, for he seemed weak. It could not be that the contrast of his pallor with the vigor of the others was newly getting her down, because they were all old friends and saw one another constantly back in Virginia.

Also, she herself had fully developed general's-wife killer instincts; it was a pity she hadn't been able to use them like these other women, real generals' wives. In Saint-Pantaléon, I could see that Simone's skills, Frenchwoman though she was—that is to say, full of rigor and wiles—were underdeveloped compared to those of women who had spent decades as the wives of successful generals. Sally Rolfe and Cynthia Baum—even Lynne Lee— could not come up to them; her passionate resentment, the flavor of her disappointment, husband just a colonel, were too palpable.

"I could never write a book. How marvelous for you," Lynne was saying. "I'm absolutely too damn stupid and that's a fact," which seemed to mean: stupidity is exactly what's needed for book writing, bitch, and fortunately I'm too smart for that.

"I see that Willard and your husband are back. It looks like Willard won. I can always tell from the way he walks. I tell him he has to let other people beat him once in a while so they'll keep playing with him," she said.

John and Willard Lee went to shower. We ladies swam, then went with the generals into the village to look at the church.

When I came out from showering and changing at dinnertime, Simone was bringing drinks onto the patio—whatever these are called in France, I suppose *terrasses*. I helped her with the trolley of glasses while she filled the ice bucket. When she came out of the kitchen, where Cynthia Baum was putting the finishing touches on the dinner, she was literally grinding her teeth.

"The Cuisine Derby" was her only remark.

Then the interesting cuisine. The food was evolved to an obsessive pitch; luckily, the haricots verts we had brought were harmonious with Cynthia's perfect *navarin*. The company was convivial and relaxed by the end of dinner, and sat up late talking or, rather, listening to a discussion of history—all except Stuart, who went to bed before ten.

The topic of historical memory came up after the excellent dinner, when we'd gathered on the patio and the American army general Rolfe was telling about his French ancestors. His colleague, Bill Baum, was in Europe to look up his roots in Germany. The Baums and Rolfes were both retired and had the luxury of time for genealogical research.

"Some of my forebears were Huguenots from around La Rochelle," Rolfe was saying, "but some were Catholics fleeing before the Revolution. The French Revolution, I mean. Many people don't realize the extent of Catholic immigration into America, mostly into Maryland. . . ."

It was this interesting discourse, well informed and lightly given, on the subject of early immigrants to America that had prompted Simone's saying that it was unusual for Americans to take an interest in history in any form. "After they mention the Pilgrims or covered wagons, they fall silent, they know nothing."

"It's because we don't believe that ancestry matters; it's what you are yourself that counts. It's an axiom of Americanness to be self-made," said John, sturdily defensive of our supposed national classlessness and belief in possibilities.

"Americans seem to think we French are pathetic for knowing and caring so much about our background," Simone went on.

"It's easier for you because French history took place on such a small stage," said John, unfairly, I thought, since French history had bled all across Europe and even to Russia. I recognized a belligerent edge to his tone; he was evidently stung by the knowledge that though he had a covered wagon in his family tree—his own grandmother went to California in one in the 1880s—that's about as much as he knew.

Simone asked John and me about our ancestors, and was triumphant when we gave vague answers. Most Americans she'd met had no idea about anything before their own grandfathers, if that. Neither of us had thought much about them beyond a mention of Scotch-Irishness, whatever that was.

"Indifference to history," Simone sniffed. "That's why Americans seem so naïve and always invade the wrong countries."

How American we suddenly felt. It's when you're in a foreign land and someone criticizes the United States that you come to feel most American, and in my case, most midwestern, because California, where I've lived for fifty years, has never felt as much like America as Illinois does.

"Well, now, that's why we've all come to France," said General Rolfe, smoothly diplomatic, "to find out more about history and avoid the mistakes of the past." I thought I also detected a note of sarcasm pointedly meant to remind Simone of American involvement in two wars to save France. It was during the Second World War that she had met Stuart, a young American officer

come to save her. I also thought, but did not say, about how both
our fathers, John's and mine, had fought in the First World War
to save France, in 1918.

We were on our way to Italy, as I said, to a foundation where
we would work on our books. I was writing up certain travel experiences I'd had on trips with John having to do with tuberculosis and AIDS in distant places. I could have included in my
book this visit with the generals that ended so embarrassingly,
but I didn't; it was too soon to digest, really.

Since Simone's generals, William Baum and Francis Rolfe, were
both retired, they had the luxury of time for genealogical research, but they had once been famous fighting men, involved in
wars and peacetime cleanups and the training of other soldiers.
The older of the two, General Rolfe, was, apparently, a legend in
his day, called "Big Cat," or some such bellicose epithet.

The wives of the generals, Sally Rolfe and Cynthia Baum,
were also talking of the war campaigns and genealogical research.
Roots are so arbitrary, anyway, that both of the generals' ladies
had adopted, perhaps in deference to the superior rank of their
husbands, their husbands' ancestry. They were familiar with the
names of ships sailing out from La Rochelle in the seventeenth
century, and of villages in Holland where Huguenots had sheltered, and of places in Germany, which was called something else
then, where the sturdy Mennonite pig farmers and potato dig-
gers packed their painted travel trunks for the New World.

The ladies themselves could have been any old American
mélange like the rest of us there listening, except for our French
friend, Simone. She was an American citizen, but not very American. Though female lineage is apt to be surrendered with the last

name, in confrontations with Americanness, Frenchness somehow
prevails, as water puts out fire, fire burns paper, and paper soaks
up water, and so Simone had not surrendered Frenchness to her
American husband, she'd added Americanness on. Are roots arbitrary after all, or adopted?

II

FLYOVER COUNTRY

2

Moline, Pop. 34,000

It was quite a while after this visit before I realized that my French friend Simone Ward had done me a favor by challenging my lack of historical consciousness. The impulse to learn about your personal background is almost universal when you come to a certain age, and so maybe I would have come to feel it eventually. But it was our visit to the generals that set me to thinking about midwestern folk, and feeling sorry I didn't know more of those stories my aunts, all dead now, could have told me—all those secrets that go to the grave.

I had always had a slightly uneasy relation to my midwestern origins, conscious of the scorn that people in more fashionable places felt for the plump, bespectacled, respectable folks whom television interviewers like to goad into conservative expostulations about the perfidies of the outside world.

I'd also been stung by the French disdain for our American weak grasp of history. Before Simone's remark about our lack of historical memory, I had simply enjoyed the pleasurable fact that I was in France, on my way to Italy. I'd been thinking of myself as a worldly traveler, someone who felt at home in England or Samoa, a citizen of the world. But now, beside my curiosity about the past, a feeling stole in, a stab of disloyalty, an illicit and even fraudulent feeling. Was it possible I was only pretending to be comfortable in Europe when I am really an Illinois hayseed whose core of naïveté cannot be effaced?

Eventually, when we'd gone back to California, other aspects of this weekend stayed with me too, especially Simone's observation that besides our lack of historical self-confidence, Americans also have delusions of grand origins. Did I? Did the other people in my small Illinois birthplace of Moline, or my mother's little town of Watseka? Or the Iowans of the Hacklebarney region, where my father came from? I was not about to incur Simone's gleeful scorn by admitting I had been told by my aunt Henrietta that our family was descended from the Capetian kings of France, confirming her assertion that we all believe ourselves royal.

Who were our families? I had supposed they had always been in Illinois or Iowa, but of course that couldn't be literally true. There must have been the scourges or droughts, ambitions, failures, or promises long ago that took the people to small Illinois towns—reasons that were now vanished beyond recollection, just like the beautiful elms that once shaded their streets, then gave up and died of Dutch elm disease, so that no one could imagine them now. It was too late, I thought, to learn very much about our particular history; my parents and all their siblings were dead and I had no one to ask.

On our visit to Simone and Stuart, a violent fire had recently swept through the south of France, driven by the mistrals, burning houses and vineyards and the shrubbery of the low hills, lending to the properties an aspect of forlorn defeat and an acrid odor people said would take months to dispel, as after a war. Maybe it was this burned and ruined smell that blighted our visit, which was to end in chagrin, but it had invoked too a pleasant nostalgia: the smoky air of Provence had put me in mind of the burning of the shocks in Illinois cornfields.

Every year, from 1907 until 1992, the *Chicago Tribune,* the once mighty organ and arbiter of midwestern belief and man⸗ ners, saluted Indian summer with a pair of drawings and a little story by John T. McCutcheon. A boy and his grandfather sit by a bonfire on the edge of a field at sundown, looking at the corn shocks gathered in the fields. As they gaze in the lowering dark at the smoke from the fires, the shapes of the stacks seem to be tepees, and gradually the two observers come to see the ghosts of Indian braves dancing around them.

The old man says, "Lots o' people say it's just leaves burnin', but it ain't. It's the campfires, an' th' Injuns are hoppin' 'round 'em t'beat the old Harry. You jest come out here tonight when the moon is hangin' over the hill off yonder an' the harvest fields is all swimmin' in the moonlight, an' you can see the Injuns and the tepees jest as plain as kin be."

I'm not sure why the *Trib* dropped this traditional feature— maybe people lost patience with the folksy tone of the grandfa⸗ ther, or resented McCutcheon's rendition of the local Illinois accent, or considered it politically incorrect to mention Injuns.

I partly resented Simone's scorn for our American genealogi⸗ cal ignorance, our national feeling that human history started in 1776, because there was some truth to it that we ignore every⸗ thing that came earlier. But up to a point I did know where I was from—Moline, Illinois. A pleasant place, surrounded by corn⸗ fields, I had always longed to get out of.

A child born in the Midwest, especially in the days before television, is bound to feel herself and everyone around her to be marooned in those waving fields of corn, stranded far from any ocean or shore, far from other continents, far from the hun⸗ gry Chinese children we could dig down to. Growing up along

the Mississippi River in Moline, I was a child who felt that the
great world was somewhere else. In towns like Moline, or Bloomfield, or Chenoa and Watseka, where my aunts and uncles lived,
or in many another midwestern town, you sense yourself to be,
and are, landlocked in the center of an immense continent, a
thousand or more miles in any direction from any ocean, and I
thought I wasn't likely ever to see an ocean.

On a recent trip back, with one of Moline's iconic farm machines

How to capture the landlocked American midwestern child
dreaming of the sea, and a feeling of vestigial belonging, via the
sea, to somewhere afar, of which we had almost lost the collective
memory? It's true the Mississippi runs to the Gulf of Mexico,
symbolizing escape, if you could get a boat and float down it to
places I would never go—how could a child like me go anywhere?

Up it had come Father Marquette, bringing France with him, still seen in place names like Moline, or Joliet, or Des Moines, or La Platte. But Mr. Gordon, our junior high school language teacher, told us not to bother learning the *tu* form of French verbs, as we probably would never meet a French person—let alone know him well enough to use it, he would say with a wink that was lost on us.

The Midwest was and is a farming region, one of the three most fertile places on earth, equaled only by some parts of the Yangtze River Delta and somewhere in Argentina. The area is watered by a system of rivers, with bluffs and hills around them to break the flatness of the fields. The soil is sooty black, like the coal and other minerals that underlie it, and the acres and acres of yellowing cornstalks at harvest time, with huge green harvesting machines like alien space insects moving through them, are sights of astonishing beauty.

Midwesternness might not interest people from other places. New Yorkers, as we know, are really interested only in New York, in what their ancestors were escaping or how they got there on the storm tossed seas, or their bad experiences on Ellis Island or on some evil continent elsewhere. Midwesterners lack a peculiarity or distinction, have no regional characteristic by which to attract or be described. Southerners had belles and plantations and their myths of gentility. The East had sophistication and influence and skyscrapers; the West had cowboys and scenic grandeur. Our very topography condemned us: flat. Plain on the plains. We were never a tourist destination.

In my childhood, none of my relatives had been anywhere else; tales were not told about distant places, only about Bloomfield, or over to Pontiac or Muscatine or faraway Des Moines, journeys to be made by automobile on two-lane roads along farm sections, commenting on the progress of the crops, waiting for the Burma-Shave signs to unfold: "You can beat / A mile a minute / But there ain't / No future in it."

"Saunders' corn is back of ours," my aunts would judge, with satisfaction.

Farm folks, small-town folks, the family it seemed had always been around Illinois, and their great-great-grandparents too. No one thought much about where or when they'd come to the Midwest, they were just there. It comforted me little that my parents and my aunts and uncles had lived here for two hundred years, some in the same creaky, dust-moted houses their departed forebears had lived in. My doom would surely be the same.

I dreamed of escape. My mother was from another little Illinois town, Watseka, on the border with Indiana, and my father came from Bloomfield, in the Hacklebarney region of southeastern Iowa, two towns way smaller than Moline; my parents were happy where we were and thought of it as a booming big place. But my Iowan father had actually been somewhere once, nearly twenty years before I was born, and may have breathed into me my secret sedition. As a soldier in the First World War, he had been to Venice, Italy.

For him, as for many farm boys of this time, 1918, that was his first and only trip to the legendary, foreign world of Europe, and, contrary to most people's experiences of that terrible war, he seemed to have found it thrilling. Every night he read to me from my favorite book, *Let's Go 'Round the World with Bob and Betty*, by Phyllis Ayer Sowers. Two children like my brother and me were taken by a benign family friend to Tokyo, to Hawaii, to China, to Egypt, around the Horn. It begins:

"'Oh, Betty! We can't see land anywhere,' cried Bob, as he ran up the deck to the place where Betty was playing quoits with Lolita, a little Cuban girl, who was returning to Havana with her mother. There was nothing but the blue ocean all around them, as the big ship tipped slowly on the waves.'"

Father liked it as much as I did.

3

My Moline

A few years ago, someone from my Illinois hometown had passed along a book about it, *My Moline* by John Cervantes. The subtitle is *A Young Illegal Immigrant Dreams*. Only now, home in California from our visit to Simone and Stuart, did I sit down to read it.

I opened it with some trepidation. My own memories of Moline, which I had left when I was sixteen, had over the years taken on a certain configuration of a bland, sound, genial place, which I dreaded the author would refute. Instead, my recollections were confirmed, though from his very different point of view; an unusually dense and myopic child, I had been unaware that Moline had Hispanic immigrants, tracks, boxcars in which people lived, social stratifications—these things were reflected in Cervantes's account of a welcoming and benign American experience. Benign: for instance, when his brother stole an alarm clock from Frank DeJaeger's store, Mr. DeJaeger, instead of prosecuting the boy, took an interest in the family ever after. High-mindedness was not discussed as an exception to the general evil of the human character but as an example of how Moline was. Mr. Cervantes and I didn't differ in our impressions of civic goodness, though his valiant Horatio Alger history paints a more difficult beginning and a more stalwart and determined character than my own.

He was born in 1915 and arrived in Moline from Mexico with the rest of his family in 1925, lived in a boxcar, and went to

Moline High School, as I would later and where my father was the principal. John Cervantes writes he was "ashamed of having to live cooped up in a two-room boxcar," and "fantasized all kinds of dreams about digging a lovely home beneath that squalid exterior, and having the boxcar be but an entry to a magnificent subterranean home." Eventually, he became a professor, and he reports that it was the kindness and supportiveness of people in Moline, especially one or two special teachers, that made his escape possible.

I learn that fifteen years before the Cervantes family's arrival, in 1910, Moline had had the second highest per capita income in America. This would not have been true in my childhood, but perhaps reflects the continuing self-image of the town, or maybe its self-delusions, as a haven of cultivated tastes, civility, and prosperity.

To emphasize our connection with the great world of European culture, children were taken, for instance, to view Mrs. Butterworth's Tiepolo ceiling, brought over from some Italian palazzo (my father said Venetian bar, and the Tiepolo was by Diziani) in the heyday of plow manufacturing, on which rested the industrial base of the region, and of the Velie automobile factory that had so enriched the founders and then itself foundered. The descendants of John Deere, like his granddaughter Mrs. Butterworth, still resident in Moline, had cultural aspirations, perhaps even accomplishments. We children lay on our backs in her sumptuous library, lined up like corpses on a tarmac, and gazed reverently up at the frolicking putti. "Proud Moline," we were called, somewhat derisively, I assume, in the rougher river towns nearby, where, unlike in Moline, or so we believed, there were jazz musicians, brothels, and bars.

* * * * *

Moline rises from levees along the Mississippi and is generally
hilly, and wooded with oak and beech. On weather maps, the
climate is characterized as midlatitude steppe, representing a region of bitter winter cold and disagreeable summer heat that begins somewhere in Mongolia and worsens as it comes over the
pole to cover Canada and the upper American Midwest, or
maybe it starts with us. In the long winter, the rule in our house
was that if it was below zero outside (in Celsius, minus 17!), we
had to wear heavy leggings to walk to school, pulled on under our
skirts and Brownie uniforms; and as it was often below zero for
weeks on end, we wore these itchy garments for months on end,
and boots or galoshes, mittens, earmuffs, mufflers, and hats, small
padded figures clumping reluctantly along the icy sidewalks. I
see now that we had to walk everywhere because in the cold the
cars wouldn't ever start.

On my birthday at the end of April, the question for me was
whether there would still be snow on the ground. Usually there was,
but often the Spring Beautys—the first wildflowers to appear—
had begun to peek through the thinning melt, and I knew that
shortly, lilies of the valley and violets would cover our hill.

We lived at the top of a ravine, with a little brook at the bottom that wended into woodland and pastures on the edge of town.
We had a rope to swing out over the ravine, and sledded down it
in winter. Our grade school, Logan, was a couple of blocks to the
west, and when I was twelve, Calvin Coolidge Junior High School
was a twenty-minute walk to the south, its name an indication of
the political sympathies of the town.

My parents built our two-story, gabled clapboard house
when I was about five. I believe they sent for the blueprints,

Our family's "Updated Cape Cod" home

Looking at our house from the ravine

hesitating over "New England Salt Box," or "Colonial," and finally choosing "Updated Cape Cod" from a mail-order source, maybe *House Beautiful.* I can still remember the smell of sawdust, and the scary look of the open rafters as they were raised. We went each day to view the progress, and I think I can remember some of the discussions around the plans, and the tattered blueprints always preserved in a desk drawer. One feature of my mother's improvements to the plan was a long mantel, the length of the living room, incorporating bookcases, something considered quite modern in that era. Otherwise it was a pretty but basic three-bedroom house with upstairs dormer windows, a front door, side door, and door into the garage.

These were never locked. The meter reader would come in by the side door and progress directly across the kitchen to the basement, where the meters and washing machine were—it was here I found him one day upon coming home from junior high, treed by our dog Tarby. "Please, kid, call off your hound," he cried; "I've been here five hours!" It gave me a terrific feeling of power to free this adult by graciously dismissing Tarby from her duty.

The family who lives there now has enclosed the porch, which was only screened in our day, and the new people are more ambitious gardeners than we, and mow the long hillside down into the ravine. My father had contented himself with a tidy swath around the house, leaving the banks a tangle of weeds and wildflowers. "I prefer things to be natural," he claimed.

My parents were Frances and Dolph Lain. I loved them, but back then, I didn't think of them as having individuality or thoughts; I couldn't have characterized them at all. Now that they are gone, I see they could have been called acerbic, calm, and sensible, like Calvin's parents in the comic strip *Calvin and Hobbes,* and eccentric by Moline standards, if only because they were older than the parents of my friends. (When Calvin asks, "Mom, Dad, am I a gifted child?" his parents say something like "Do you think we would have paid for you?")

My parents were harmonious, or at least never quarreled in front of us. Since parents are meant to be staunch and invincible, I was aghast, twice, by finding my mother weeping—once during pregnancy when she had been advised by the doctor to eat only bananas every other day, and she was sick to tears of them, and the other when she had an unwelcome birthday, a trauma mitigated by their friends, who surprised her with a cake bearing the motto "Life Begins at Forty." Now I wonder if maybe at this crisis she had had a moment of regret about not having gone anywhere in the world beyond Moline. But she never left America or seemed to want to.

By the time I became aware of them, our parents were middle-aged, my father almost fifty. I could have described how they looked, of course: my mother five feet tall, brown-haired, and pretty; my father almost six feet, and bald, with a blond fringe. Men with hair still don't look fatherly to me. A childhood friend has told me since that she thought we lived at the summit of graciousness because my art-teacher mother guided me and my little friends in projects—carving linoleum block prints to make Christmas cards, for instance, or stringing popcorn for the tree—and (my friend's example) serving us orange slices dusted with powdered sugar and coconut. Sometimes to my immense chagrin my father would sing, in a pretty, light tenor, "Little Grey Home in the West."

After five years of being the cherished apple, I was "given" a baby brother, which my parents had read was the best way to frame it. I don't remember minding, but there is home movie footage of me pinching the poor baby, wearing an evil expression. Thomas Michael was a good natured, fat cherub with, of course, the blond, curly hair I had always wanted, and grew to be an exemplary Eagle Scout, essay prize winning sort of boy, now a doctor. Eventually his successes gave me joy, if only because of the analgesic age gap between us.

The eponymous John Deere, who died in 1886, had seen the need for plows to turn the coal colored soil of the vast prairie, and had imported workers from Scandinavia. My friends in Moline were often the children or grandchildren of those immigrants. Even in the 1940s, some of them had parents who didn't pronounce their initial *J*'s, and said *V* for *W*—a source of some hilarity for kids, their own children included, who chanted a rhyme that began "My name is Yohn Yohnson. . . ." It made even the Swedes laugh that the proprietor of the automobile plant had been named Will Velie, which his employees would all pronounce "Vill Weelie."

These immigrants must have brought with them some of the cooperative and generous social attitudes we associate with Scandinavia today, to create the general welcoming mood in Moline, the same mood that John Cervantes felt. Nostalgic at Christmas, the Old Country grandparents required their Americanized kids to eat mysteriously awful, Old Country lutefisk, a sort of marinated dried fish, and *strömming*, made of fermented herring, much to their misery. Was there an ordinance forbidding Saint

Lucia headdresses of lighted candles in December? I never knew
for sure, for we were not Lutheran, but we heard tales of girls who
had had to be doused with buckets of water. Neither were we
Swedish, which I mournfully regretted, especially not being
blond and tall like most of my classmates. It seemed that most
names in our town ended in some Scandinavian suffix. In my
small Logan school class there were a Swanson, two Carlsons, a
Morhausen, a Samuelson, a Tomlinson, a Nordstrom, an Effland,
a Hoagland. . . . Only Marjorie Young, Lynn Edwards, and I, Diane Lain, were without Scandinavian last names, and Marjorie
and Lynn might have had Swedish mothers.

Besides Swedes, the ethnic group we were most conscious of
was Native American. Though there were no reservations in
Illinois—the farmland being too valuable—local places and
parks were named after Chief Black Hawk and other Indians
who had battled the settlers for the territory along the river; and
there was much emphasis, in elementary school, on acorn tea,
and baskets woven from twigs. Towns around were called Ot-
tumwa or Keokuk after Indian tribes or figures—Watseka, Chenoa, Ottawa, Oskaloosa, Kankakee, Kewanee, and so on.

There were not, however, any Native American kids whom I
knew, and there were very few African Americans. The two or
three in our school were superior beings; I was especially in awe
of the handsome Dave McAdams, a boy a few grades ahead of
me, who was the quarterback and the valedictorian, and had an
outstanding singing voice. He would be invited or hired to sing
in our church from time to time, after some debate about the
propriety of this, not because of his race but because he was believed to be a Baptist. Then there were Cal and Flip Anders, two
inspiringly tall brothers who played basketball and earned extra

money washing ceilings, and Evans Grigsby, younger, just a plain little kid.

In general, because minorities were so few in number, they were fostered with a certain community feeling of self-satisfied rectitude, though it's possible we children were shielded from attitudes of prejudice the way we were shielded from rude words: "mackerel-snapper" for Catholics was the only ethnic slur I ever remember hearing. (The *n* word was considered improper but occurred in *Huckleberry Finn,* and in "Eeny, meeny, miny, moe" until someone thought of replacing it with "tiger.") Basically I had never heard anyone swear except for the occasional "damn" or "hell" until I was about sixteen, when fat Robert Nourse, coming along on his bicycle, leaned in on my friends and me and, with a daring glitter in his eye, called us "fucking monsters." Then we knew we had heard a powerful, forbidden word, whatever it meant.

That was as shocking as anything got in Moline, though once, on the playground pavement of our Calvin Coolidge Junior High School, someone did draw a rude chalk outline of our principal, Mr. Congdon, with a ten-foot penis. This didn't actually shock, because we had received thorough explanations about sexual reproduction in a seventh-grade lecture series by Dr. Murphy, carefully overseen by our mothers, who also attended the lectures to verify the accuracy and wholesomeness of the content.

So we knew everything about the penis, though we had not seen one. I had discounted the rosebud protuberance sported by my little brother. Once Barbara Bopf and I, walking home at nightfall, were passed by a flasher, but, in the gloom, did not really understand what the indistinct white form was at the front of his pants; we thought perhaps a handkerchief was dangling from his belt.

My nearsightedness was to impede my early understanding of lots of things. Once, during a football game (for these were weekly events from earliest childhood), I was sent into the field house for something, and there surprised a naked boy on his way to the showers. But I couldn't really describe what I had seen to my disappointed, brotherless friends, not even his identity.

4

Myopia

If you were a nearsighted child, you will remember getting your first pair of glasses, on a day that changed your life in two (or more) ways. First, what an amazing revelation to see the dazzling world, all the way across the street! The blackboard! The ball hurtling toward you! At the same time, you knew you were now linked to a mechanical device, an appliance, an impediment, a symbol of limitation and imperfection. You were no longer suffi, cient unto yourself.

I think it was my second-grade teacher, Miss Garretson, who noticed me leaning forward, or squinting, or misbehaving— something that caused her to alert my parents that perhaps I didn't see very well. Maybe it isn't brattiness or stupidity that makes her so wiggly and talkative! See how she scrunches up her eyes.

I can still bring back the tobacco smell of the eye doctor leaning closely to peer with his strange instrument into the in, sides of my eyes, sending eye images bouncing around my skull, and the dilation drops and the paper shade to wear afterward. And the great clumsy pair of test glasses, like an oxen yoke upon my nose, with sliding lenses to be pushed in and out until I could see the letters on a chart. Is this better? Or is that? It seems strange that this method of refraction hasn't changed very much in the ensuing seventy years.

I went with my father to pick up my new glasses when they were ready, and still remember my stupefaction at seeing all the way down the street, at how bright and clear the world was. It was shock as much as delight, that so much seen meant so much to be seen, and such a range of pitfalls previously unseen. None of the disadvantages had yet occurred to me, it was simple aston-ishment. "I didn't know you were supposed to see way over there," I said. But my father right then and there in the car be-gan to cry, tears of remorse to think they'd never noticed any-thing wrong with me.

5

Pastimes

What did people do in Moline? My parents were teachers, and my father was principal of the high school. Good teachers and schools, the several country clubs and golf courses, and a professional basketball team reflected the true cultural interests of the community—that and high school football, which was the dominant spectator sport and preoccupation. My father had played football in college and was a sometime and part-time coach, so maybe football interest was especially keen in our house, but my memory is that our parents, we kids, and all our and their friends went to the games, sometimes Friday nights, sometimes Saturday afternoons, from grade school on. Somewhere I still have the furlined "stadium boots" I was given when my feet were big enough, even so bought several sizes too large so I could keep growing. You froze at these games but didn't mind, and if you got too cold you could run around, stomping your stadium boots behind the bleachers till you could feel your feet again. I thought weekend football games were an intrinsic part of natural life.

Members of the football team were admired above all other students, and when we got to adolescence, my friends and I would have given anything to be asked out by a football player. The football players were somehow older-seeming, "experienced," and maybe not quite what our mothers would approve of, though eventually I had the satisfaction of having as my best college friend, when I had mysteriously washed up in Salt Lake City, the quarterback of the Utah team—like me, an English major and

not a Mormon. As outcasts, we studied together and walked together to classes—I was married by then and heavily pregnant
with my first child, and so incurred puzzled looks from jealous
coeds. I admired his insouciant indifference to public speculation
about my state.

In Moline, the young, lively parents of my friend Holly went
to formal dances at the country club, but my parents, who were
older, laughed and said they couldn't imagine anything worse. My
parents laughed at the idea of country club dances, or anything
they considered pretentious, but I secretly thought their derision
was a form of rationalization for things we couldn't afford. Surely
anyone would dress up in black lace and go to dances if they
could? I was acutely aware that some people had more money
than we, and I cared about this much more than my parents did,
though I didn't lack for anything, except a canopy bed. Such a
bed represented glamour and possibility, things to be made possible when I grew up and went somewhere else.

I had the common childhood fantasy of actually being someone else's little girl, dropped by mischance into this unsuitably
harmonious and monotonous town. I felt that Holly's parents
were way more glamorous than mine. They called their daughter
"Holl-Doll." They had cocktails every night at five-thirty, in
Hollywood-style glasses on stems, like Nick and Nora in *The
Thin Man.* When the drinks came out on the silver tray, it was
the signal for me to go home, across the driveway. Because she was
an only child, Holl-Doll had many possessions I didn't, especially
an Early American bedroom set; but neither of us had a canopy
bed, our passionate dream.

Even I, budding little snob, though, could see what was comic
about one of my classmates who would say, when being driven

home by my father in our old Chevrolet, "Just let me out there, at the house with the two Cadillacs." This family was whispered to have changed its name from something Polish or German and hard to pronounce, and changing your name was certainly looked down upon, but was thought to go along with this unbecoming materialism.

The father in the two-Cadillac family was a doctor, but not our doctor. When you got sick in our family you had Dr. Arp. Babies were delivered by Dr. Sloan—at least I was, and so was my friend the late Theophilus Brown, the painter, born twenty years before me. The dentist was Dr. Streed, who didn't really think Novocain was necessary most of the time. Dr. Arp lived a few doors away, at the corner of Sixteenth Avenue and Twenty-ninth Street. Can I be correct in remembering that the Arps had a chauffeur? It hardly seems possible in our middle-class neighborhood, nonetheless I think it was so, a chauffeur with one name, like Hampton. My friend Holly's grandfather certainly had one, Louis, but since Mr. Nelson owned a factory, it seems more plausible. We loved swan-ning around in the back of Hermie's brown Packard on the way to dancing class.

We had doctors for physical ailments, but there was not much emphasis on the problems of the mind—perhaps these were in-frequent. It was occasionally made known that Mrs. So-and-so was driving to Iowa City to see a psychiatrist, or that a troubled kid was seeing a "counselor" in Davenport, across the river, where such people were. But some sympathetic scorn attached to this; Moline was not oriented to troubles of the spirit. A talking-to usu-ally sufficed. Perhaps people actually did confide in their doctors or ministers, the way magazines enjoined you to do; or perhaps they stoically soldiered on. There were helpful columns of advice in the *Chicago Tribune* that my mother sometimes clipped out and consulted when it came time to talk about a new baby, or the birds and the bees.

In Moline, you knew not only your friends' parents but very often also their grandparents, all one-named: Holly had Hermie and Nana and Gammie, the Martin family next door had Porpor and Mormor, and so on. I had no grandparents to present to my friends, and only a dim memory of my mother's father, Grandfather Elder, with his lovely white hair, and my father's mother, Grandma Lain, already in her nineties when I was born and somewhat remote from the late offspring of her already middle-aged tenth child.

Do people play cards now the way they used to, now that they have video games and DVDs? One of my earliest memories is of being given a pack of cards by my father and directed to sort them according to suits, and then according to numbers, and to recognize the face cards, and put them all in order. Starting from simple games like war and happy families, we went on to rummy, then gin rummy, and a game called pitch, a vestige of the eighteenth-century piquet, which my father played with his brothers. In their childhood, ten kids in rural Iowa, they played furtively after lights-out, because their parents were sternly opposed to gambling (as well as to drink). Card games were as much a part of Moline life as golf was for my parents and other parents, and aunts and uncles, and everyone, and throughout the whole history of civilization as far as I knew, at least for people with any leisure time at all, before television. I especially liked cribbage, so dynamic, with its board and little pegs leaping from hole to hole.

My parents played bridge, poker, and gin with their friends, and my mother had two afternoon bridge clubs. Bridge playing required a lot of special equipment and incited much passion. You had card tables that folded and were put up, and these were covered by special fancy square linen cloths secured at the corners; there were nut cups, ashtrays, little pencils, and special score pads. Eventually, we children had bridge lessons, along with golf lessons—things my parents thought indispensable for correct adult life. Otherwise, what would you do with yourself down the years, how would you get along?

Kids also played games like Parcheesi and Monopoly, and outdoor ones like croquet and touch football. On summer nights we would dart barefooted across the lawns in our nightgowns, and in winter we sledded down our hill. Eventually, we had dancing classes and mixers at school. I read a lot, and the family listened together to certain radio programs, like *The Fred Allen Show*. My parents admired Bing Crosby and Bob Hope. My favorite was a comedian named Henry Morgan. We could have stepped out of a Norman Rockwell illustration.

Fran and Dolph were a little older than their friends, and their core bridge and golf group consisted of the next-door neighbors (the Martins), people down the street (the Gills), a stockbroker named Malcolm Bosse, and his wife, Thelma. (Their son Malcolm junior was my idol, and eventually became a distinguished novelist.) The Bosses, Martins, Gills, and Lains made two tables for bridge, though they sometimes played poker instead—and always for money, small stakes. My parents and their friends were all fond of one another, but I would overhear Fran and Dolph joking with the Martins about Thelma Bosse's wild bids, or with the Bosses about Jim Martin's drinking. They all drank quite a bit, highballs or martinis, and guests sometimes had to be seen home, but this was only down the street, and on foot.

Dorrie Martin was a handsome Swedish woman, and the three Martin daughters were all beautiful blondes, which was painful for a small, skinny, nondescript neighbor child like me, with fat brown braids. I think Jim Martin and Buford Gill were some kind of Deere and Company executives, as were many of the fathers in Moline. None of the moms worked. My mother, who had come to Moline as an art teacher, had been obliged in the custom of the day to stop teaching when she got married, though she sometimes substituted when a "real" art teacher got sick. Mr. Martin, Malcolm Bosse, and Bufe Gill presumably went to their offices each day, which was not interesting to children. But my father had a teacher's schedule, free in the summers and in the afternoons after three, so that my memories of him were as someone who didn't work at all; and since my uncles, except for Uncle Bill, didn't work either in any nine-to-five discernible way—they were mostly farmers or landholders who didn't put their own hands to the plow—I can't say I was shown a strong example of people enduring a daily grind. Grown-up people seemed to do what they liked, which was mostly playing golf.

When I was nineteen, already a married woman, I had to get an eight-to-five job, in the UCLA library, to put my husband through medical school, and this constraint—the adult reality of having to work and follow a path—had never before occurred to me. I'd never imagined that life would require me to have to go to work every day. Working was such a shock to me and so against the grain that I dwindled to weigh eighty-eight pounds. I've managed to avoid jobs ever since, though I've toiled at my writing, which appears to others as a form of play, and at being a professor, which, though it's hard, seems to strike others as easy, and isn't nine to five.

It would seem that despite our impressions of free will, we are controlled by genetics or by some hereditary caste system, so that members of a family stick to the same general path. My particular family, down through the generations, to my utmost regret, spawned mostly housewives and farmers, doctors, schoolteachers, and the odd minister—that is to say, no businessmen, no musicians or millionaires, no glamorous criminals or ne'er-do-wells, except Uncle Jack. He was a wanderer, dead before I was born, a cardplayer, my father said.

6

Economies

Though money was never discussed in our family, my brother and I were aware that we weren't particularly well off, and that our parents were careful. However, we were much like everyone we knew, and didn't dwell on our economies. Mother sewed my clothes, and Mike and I had correct but not lavish allowances. Because our family watched our pennies, the occasional new material object was a matter of thrilling novelty—a bike or desk, or decoder ring you'd sent off for.

But my brother and I kept wondering: Were we poor? Did my mother have to sew my dresses or did she just like to? Though money was never mentioned, an attitude toward it was implied: it would be somehow tacky to do something you didn't enjoy just for the money. The corollary was that if you did, the money wouldn't make you happy. My parents had both come from a whole tradition of making things, which is also a form of play, as the best things are, and until I began to write these recollections, I may not have fully realized what a sheltered nineteenth-century world Moline still was in the 1940s.

Despite my parents' scorn of materialism, some of my happiest memories concerned material possessions—particular objects that overwhelmed me with proprietary joy, like my stuffed panda bear from the Brookfield Zoo gift shop (that I still have). Once, through some form of enterprise—maybe only pasting green stamps in the books that collected in the kitchen drawer—I earned the right to an item of merchandise, and after much poring over the catalog, I chose a radio; it was a tiny Arvin with a tinny sound, but strong enough to get the programs I liked—*Jack Armstrong, The Lone Ranger, The Henry Morgan Show, Amos 'n' Andy,* and the *Grand Ole Opry* from as far away as Nashville. It was my favorite possession, and a link to the great world.

In some ways, our family life was a scene of parallel play, as it would have been disapprovingly described by my children's nursery school teachers—people side by side, not "interacting" but calling to one another from wherever they were, involved in personal projects rather than group ones. Father would be at his basement workbench, mother soaking the wicker laid out beside a chair she was caning the seat of, my brother and I in our rooms or in our secret hideaway on the closet shelf. I would be making paper dolls or playing with my button collection. These antique buttons from Watseka had names and personalities, and I made them act out stories. I had dolls, but preferred this more abstract and portable cast of characters. I still have the buttons, but, alas, they've reverted to an inert state of buttonness, and I can't remember their names.

In his basement workshop my father had the ancient lathe he had inherited from Grandfather Elder, and other tools he made things with—he sawed black walnut shells into thin slices my mother made jewelry out of. Once someone gave him a lump of mammoth tusk. I can still smell the burning ivory, like scorching tooth or bone, as he shaped bits of it on his lathe. I have china painted by my great-aunt Lottie, and a doll bed turned on the same lathe by my Elder grandfather, and many quilts and oil paintings by Mother and various aunts.

My mother was adept and fearless in all crafts, and had her own little tool kit of coping saw, leather punch, and other tools, and special stretchers to cane chairs or upholster them, and she took classes to learn unfamiliar accomplishments like hat making and tailoring. Some of these interests were transmitted to me—I know how to shrink a sleeve with a press cloth to fit an armhole; I know some interfacing lore, and how to knit and quilt and do decoupage; I can do all that and more, though not as well as she. Eventually, like lots of elderly people, my parents got television and subsided to watching golf matches and Oprah, but always with knitting or whittling on their laps.

Alas, we were not musical, though my mother's Watseka family had an attic stuffed with musical instruments, including a harp played by Aunt Henrietta; and in the Civil War (I eventually learned), my great-grandfather had led a band to inspire the soldiers of the Thirty-third Illinois Infantry. Mother retained the ability to play the ukulele, and could sing vaguely racy songs, like one about Minnie the Mermaid:

Down among the corals, Minnie lost her morals
Gee but she was good to me. . . .

In our midwestern accents we sang along: "Minny's the night I spent with Minnie. . . ."

For a while I took violin lessons on an instrument from the attic of Watseka. We were playing Tchaikovsky's *Marche Slave* in the Moline children's orchestra when word came of the victory in Europe, and as I remember, I gave up the violin after that, as if the country had no more need of my efforts. I'm sure it was a relief to my parents.

I was eventually to learn that Moline was somewhat culturally deprived compared to big cities, say, New York, with its greater symphonies and operas and theaters, or even Chicago, with its architecture and museums like the Art Institute, where my mother had gone to college, but it had plausible equivalents and lesser versions of all these things. There was actually a Tri City Symphony; it was just that our family did not attend it. When my aunt Ruth gave me an LP record of the *Moonlight Sonata*, I was shattered with surprise and yearning for more such music. I saved up to buy the *1812 Overture*, and began to listen to the Metropoli tan Opera broadcasts on Saturday mornings and often knew the answers to the quizzes at intermission. I owned Beethoven's Fifth Symphony, subscribed for from a classical record club that sent you the first one free. There were other cultural institutions, lesser versions of things a bigger place might have; there was a museum in Davenport where I took art lessons, and another museum, my favorite, called A Little Bit O' Heaven, that had been founded by the son of the inventor or éminence grise of chiropractors, B. J. Palmer. It was a rock grotto, and in it was a giant Buddha, alliga tors, and a motto:

Is life worth living? That depends on the liver.

7

Books

I wouldn't say my parents were intellectuals, but they were great readers, even if the adult conversation in our house was mostly about someone's golf handicap or unexpected conditions on the seventh green. People read more books in those days. At home we had classics like *Moby-Dick*, or *The Forty Days of Musa Dagh*, and unexpected exotica like *Mademoiselle de Maupin*, a mildly shocking French novel probably left over from one of Mother's college courses, and *The Decameron* with the naughty parts in Latin, sending me fruitlessly to the dictionary, where *cunnus* was defined unhelpfully as "a cunnus." There were the monthly arrivals of novels from The Literary Guild and Book-of-the-Month Club.

Luckily for its citizens, Moline had a Carnegie Library, in the form of a Greek temple. We must hope that Andrew Carnegie is having his reward in heaven, as my aunts would have put it, for the great good work he did in building libraries in these little towns all over America. Michael Dirda, the critic, writing in the *Times Literary Supplement* (London), recounts reading Dumas's *The Count of Monte Cristo* as a boy, and seeing in that "great parable about the power of learning and education" the lesson that one could escape from a midwestern town and join a world of high culture "through disciplined effort." That's what I saw in it too, my favorite book for a long time. I wonder if Dirda's was a Carnegie Library like mine.

My mother dropped me off there on Saturday mornings to spend three hours browsing and amassing a pile of books to read

during the week. I read my way through the "100 Greatest Novels," except for a few the library didn't have, and *Madame Bovary*,
which the librarian didn't think suitable for my age. I read all the
novels of Rafael Sabatini and of Captain Marryat, and of Nord-
hoff and Hall. I most loved the works of Alexander Dumas and
adventure stories, preferably with ships and swords. Sea tales are
what I loved most. Tales of captains, pirates, boys shanghaied.

Girls were never shanghaied, but it took me a long time to
understand that this romantic fate wasn't likely to be mine; there
was nothing to lend desirable drama to my future. In my gender-
neutral imagination, I was the protagonist, in my hammock or on
deck when the pirates were spotted on the horizon, or when the
rough mate with his eye patch went amok on the bridge. Captain
Blood, Captain Ahab, Captain Bligh, Captain Paradise (a Canadian captain, celebrated in song, who turned out to have carried
my own ancestor to these shores!). Sometimes the parents of my
friends would quiz me about my captains, and smile encourag-
ingly at the things this freaky little girl knew about Moby Dick
and Ahab. The books in childhood are the ones that can point
your life toward something, and though, in the case of a puny
midwestern girl, becoming a pirate was not a realistic goal, it took
a long time for me to relinquish that hope.

Eventually I would devour contemporary novels mostly set in
New York, about fleeing Russia, rough crossings, tenement life,
red diapers, and jails, but not until after I had already despaired
that I could overcome the disadvantages of perfectly nice parents, not being Jewish, and living in this boring little river town
where nothing ever happened, everyone was a Republican except
one boy in our class, Richard Cox, and the tallest building was

the twelve-story LeClaire Hotel, as it was in John Cervantes's day and still is.

You hear nowadays that these small cities and towns in the Midwest are hotbeds of meth labs and speed. Can that be true? I recently asked a friend who also grew up in Moline (the painter Stephanie Peek) if she thought Moline had been a sheltered place, and she said, "Are you kidding? It was Brigadoon." Though it is true that daring kids in Moline would try smoking locoweed, a noxious hallucinogen that grows in Illinois ditches, and an old American tradition, judging from Louisa May Alcott's story about the Massachusetts young people who got stoned and went sailing.

Talking of Louisa May Alcott, though I liked swashbuckling adventure stories, I didn't like the girls' books, for instance *Little Women*, that aunts, teachers, and the parents of friends pressed on me. I suspected some social conspiracy, some agenda that would impede my wish to go to sea, or, at least, west.

No one ever thought of going eastward. My mother, in the twenties, had gone as far away as Chicago, to the Art Institute. She seldom said much about it, but had kept all her art books, which I loved to look at; and she had a boyfriend from those days who stopped to visit us once in Moline, where we lived, on his way to take up his post as the ambassador to Russia. This improbable interface with the great world beyond impressed me with wistful, disloyal longings. Disloyally, I wished my father would be ambassador to Russia, instead of high school principal in Moline, so we could live in Moscow or Tashkent.

Among the pictures in Mother's art books were many beloved images, including one, *The Age of Innocence*, by Sir Joshua Reynolds, that she cut out and framed. It showed a sweet, docile little girl with a hair ribbon, and I found her sweetness and curls vaguely admonitory. Behind the languorous nudes of Titian were castled landscapes, distant and radiant, and it was those I longed for. I especially loved Titian's *Venus of Urbino*, with its mysterious kneeling figure in the background, and a cute little dog—though it seemed rude the way Venus was grabbing her crotch, as children were told not to do; my mother said it was because the artist didn't want to depict pubic hair.

Urbino was in distant Italy, and—to think—my own father had been to Italy and France! My favorite parts of *Let's Go 'Round the World with Bob and Betty* took place in Venice, where "the gondolier pushed off from the marble steps in front of the station and headed down the Grand Canal. . . ." The thrilling prospect my own father had seen, and I barely hoped to see, but how?

III

EIGHTEENTH-CENTURY BEGINNINGS

8

How We All Descend from Greatness

I had not forgotten Simone Ward's merriment about how all Americans believe they are descended from royalty. We denied that people had such beliefs, but her assertion proved to be true: it seems to be part of our American national self-image that we all have a fancy connection to the past. This was borne out by asking my friends, and almost every single one of us has been told about distinguished, even royal, forebears. People who came in the early days, whether from Europe, Latin America, or Africa, often brought with them as legend, or in family records, a tradition of some grander ancestor—a chieftain, great Talmudic scholar, famous musician, leader, duke, or academic, someone out of the ordinary, back somewhere on the family tree. I assume this is still true for families no matter when they arrive—at least they will have a talented and famous uncle, notable eccentric, or someone very, very wicked. According to Alice Kaplan's amusing book *Dreaming in French,* when Jacqueline Bouvier went to Paris in her junior year at Vassar, she took with her the family story that they were descended from French aristocrats—though, according to Kaplan's sources, they were just French tradesmen.

My parents didn't emphasize ancestral myths, and as far as I could make out, our family was nothing at all; we had no ethnic or Old Country recollections to lend color to family reminiscences—how indeed could I ever become a writer? We were Default Americans, plump, mild, and Protestant, people whose ancestors had come ashore God knew when and had lost interest in keeping

track of the details, though my Watseka aunts had documents
entitling them to be members of the Princess Wach⁄e⁄kee chapter
of the Daughters of the American Revolution, which they enthu⁄
siastically were, along with most of the other ladies in town.

They had also preserved the brief memoirs I've mentioned,
written by great⁄grandmothers, one of them meditating a divorce,
one preoccupied with piety and the consciousness of sin. I would
come to find both fascinating, as people are apt to do when they
come to their Roots time of life. "Your great⁄grandfather was
Cousin to the king of France," wrote Emily Cossitt to her cousin
Catharine in 1876. Cousin Emily strikes a very American note
when she describes how she and Catharine Perkins, to whom she's
writing, are not only related to the king of France, "we are also
related to a Cole family from Farmington, Ct. He was of English
descent and nearly allied to the house of Stuart and the unfortu⁄
nate Mary, Queen of Scots." And Catharine's father, named plain
John Perkins, descended from "the younger son of a Noble fam⁄
ily" too. These ladies, Emily and Catharine, lived more than a
century later than the ancestor who first came to America, but
he was in some sense within their living memory, as they repeat
the stories they heard as girls, told by people who almost remem⁄
bered him—especially their uncle Bliss, one of a Stebbins family
of rustic Puritans who figured among the 1704 Deerfield captives
(which I will get to)—and reckoned themselves descended from
kings called Hadding, Hothbrod, Wiglaf, Uffe, Frode, and C.
Roric Slyngband. The Stebbinses traced their ancestry back to
818 B.C., a remarkable feat of genealogical persistence! The idea of
some aristocratic connection, while reflecting on the present de⁄
graded state of things, suggests the hope of eventual salvation, as
in religion, a future time when merit will finally win out.

The individual moments in each child's development when he dreams that he is the child of superior beings, because he couldn't possibly be the child of the hopeless people who claim him, also seems to characterize us collectively: our real American origins lie with long·gone kings. Our presidents are the imperfect parents we turn against. Freud called the sense people have that they are really the children of someone grander and more im· portant than the imperfect parents they have "the family ro· mance." For himself he imagined a tribal tradition in which a royal Egyptian—Moses—was his forebear. More than half of American presidents have been found by determined genealo· gists to be distant cousins of the English royal family, or de· scended from English and Irish royalty—Barack Obama most recently. "Obama's mother, Ann, brought to his gene pool a de· scent from the 17th·century plantation owner Mareen Duvall," said genealogist Robert Barrett, according to *People* magazine. "She is an ancestor of the Duchess of Windsor." And Obama, ac· cording to Barrett, also "has a rich mixture of European ancestors, including the early medieval kings of England and Scotland, a signatory of the Magna Carta, and, for good measure, an Irish emigrant from County Offaly."

There's a vast library of books about Americans' national royal connections: Browning's *Americans of Royal Descent* and *The Magna Charta Barons and Their American Descendants,* and *Plantagenet Ances· try of Seventeenth-Century Colonists,* to name a few. And there's quite an industry of devising family crests for Americans, or ostensibly researching the ones that have been lost. Our royal stories are often combined with a persecution story—accounts of Huguenots, Pil· grims, pogroms, slavery, wrongs of every kind that of course really happened. Among picturesque victims, Americans identify with

Marie Antoinette; you wouldn't want to think you were descended from the horrible, bloodthirsty Robespierre or Simon Legree.

Our national mythology telling us that individually, and therefore collectively, we are descended from greatness might also explain our national delusions of grandeur, beliefs that encourage a sense of privilege, the mind-set that finally impedes us by insisting that we are the best country even when the facts are otherwise, about our freedom, our health (we are number forty-two in the world in health), our roads, our crime rate, our lack of trains, our declining per capita income; even our standard of living is not ranked best. On many measures, we are far from the top—but how can that be? We've been programmed to think otherwise. America's royal connections have fostered our belief in our exceptionalism, a tradition the opposite of, say, the Australians, who came to feel it was chic to have a convict ancestor, the lower and more desperate the better: anyone kicked out of England was someone they wanted.

Cousin Emily ends her letter on a plaintive and more realistic note, hoping there was some way of getting their fair share of a spread of Cossitt Canadian lands: "This regal ancestry don't amount to much when we are in need of more bread and butter, for everyone ought in this republican form of government to stand on their own merit, and be appreciated for their talented head or kindly heart."

That's what we all believe, or say we do.

9

Ranna

Such is the geography of our continent that all American stories begin with someone crossing an ocean to come here, even Native Americans, who are thought to have come from Asia via Siberia. As we learned in grade school, very often the reason people came to America was religious (closely connected to political) persecution that drove them to leave wherever they were; but sometimes they were drawn here by the wish to proselytize. Missionary work and Utopian religious schemes brought settlers from Germany and England; little nuns, expendable younger daughters, were shipped out from France to Canada to convert the Indians, and younger sons became priests or soldiers. Then there were plain village girls and women convicted of prostitution or theft, recruited to come marry the trappers and farmers. The first people who came, for whatever reason, were usually fleeing, like the Pilgrims, and this means that the people who eventually went out to the Midwest likely had families with some traditions of flight.

But most American tales start with an arrival. Where to start in any history is arbitrary, given the exponential number of forebears a person living now actually has, and to trace one or two lines means ignoring the others. It's inevitable that the ancestors who get remembered were those who were male, articulate, or distinguished, whose names appear in public records, people who conscientiously registered at city hall and were entered in family Bibles. This story starts with some people named Cosset,

because their story can be taken as exemplary—lots of mid,
western families had similar beginnings, coming down from peo,
ple fleeing England or France.

The Cossets were regular folks with family Bibles and a
penchant for saving letters and deeds, and providentially not
throwing them out on their westward migration, giving us these
quick glimpses of an unhappy maiden or an anguished young fa,
ther ill or in debt. If it weren't for their historian impulses, they'd
be forgotten, but the first arrival, Ranna Cosset, got himself into
history books through his particular misfortune.

With apologies to all the unsung others, Ranna's story, to
stand for many others, begins arbitrarily with him, René Cossé or
Cosset, a young Frenchman setting sail for Canada from France
in 1711 with his brother François, in their tricornered hats and
bright military uniforms, on board the *Neptune*. Trying to under,
stand what prompted young Frenchmen to go to North America
in 1711 has given me a good deal of sympathy for professional
historians, who are expected to know things and not encouraged
to speculate.

Why had this particular young man of twenty,one set out for
the dangerous New World? Why had he undertaken a precari,
ous sea voyage of uncertain duration in a small sailing vessel
with stuffy quarters belowdecks for all but the first,class passen,
gers, a crew no doubt about to mutiny (judging from the usual
sea stories), horrible rations of beans and salt pork, wormy bread,
no vegetables? There were rats, maybe seasickness the whole
way. People often didn't survive the trip. What drove any of
them to sign on for such hardship?

We can only speculate: He might have been a simple soldier
going to serve in the colonies. If he was an aristocrat coming

to America in 1711 (as some descendants like to claim), that would imply he was either an adventurous younger son or, more likely, a Huguenot, though family tradition has him a Catholic who instantly converted to Protestantism for the love of Ruth Porter, a maiden he met in Massachusetts when he was a prisoner there.

If the Cossés, or Cossets—for people spelled their last names every which way—were Huguenots, his flight would have been the effect of the revocation by Louis XIV in 1685 of the Edict of Nantes, a law that until then had ensured religious tolerance for persecuted Protestants. It's said the king canceled it at the urging of Madame de Maintenon, his pious second wife, and it was too bad he did. Protestant fears of renewed slaughter launched a vast brain-drain exodus to England, Holland, and the New World, and explains one tradition that says Ranna attended Oxford, for many French Protestants had fled first to England.

On the other hand, by 1711 French Catholics had been settling in Canada for a century, and certain families already had holdings there—he might simply have been emigrating to (or from) relatives in Canada, as another family story goes.

Much of what I could find about Ranna was based on the somewhat mythologized account (mentioned above) sent in 1876 to Catharine by one of her older cousins, Emily Cossitt, a daughter of the intrepid adventurer's grandson. Her letter begins, as most letters did, with the inevitably bleak report on an ailing relative. Health was a large subject in correspondence at this period, as in their lives: "Br[other] John has been sick for nearly two months, and is now so ill that his recovery is thought quite doubtful. . . ." She then recounts her and her cousin's royal connections, via this Ranna:

I fear it would take more leisure than I can now command to write volumes of biography relative to our noble family. . . . Our great-grandfather's name was Ranna (or Rene) Cossitt, pronounced Cossa. And his father's name was Ranna, who was the one that came from France and was the son of Capet Cossitt, cousin to Louis Capet, King of France. When Lafayette was here on his last visit to this country, on being introduced to my dear father, he remarked to him that his name was very familiar to him in Paris and some of his dearest friends bore that name, and doubtless [were] his relatives.

"Ranna"? Some languages didn't travel well, and French was one of them; the young traveler was trustfully setting out from France under his name of René Cossé or Cosset, only to find it quickly transmogrified to Connecticut ears as Ranna Cossitt. Faute de mieux, he took to spelling it like that. (Ranna's brother François's name underwent an even more endearing mutation, to "Franceway," a spelling he too passed on to his children, and there are still Ranna and Franceway Cossitts.) These Cossitts were typical of the people along the Eastern Seaboard who would struggle westward, hopeful, modest, industrious, leaving behind their languages, old spellings, *accents aigus.*

Ranna's arrival in America in 1711 is noted in the record of his time mainly because of his capture by the English and subsequent history:

One day on their voyage . . . the vessel in which the young men were, was taken by Capt. Mathews and brought into Middleton, Ct. as prisoners of war, these United States being then provinces of Great Britain. He, with the other prisoners of war were taken to New Haven and permitted to go

at large on his parole, that he should not go out of New
Haven until exchanged.

Some background about the British capture: whatever young
Ranna's reasons for heading to the New World from Europe in
1711, he must have been aware of the small, bloody war taking
place on the eastern coast and the adjacent seas—Queen Anne's
War, a conflict hardly mentioned by historians now. The struggle
was between Queen Anne of England and the Sun King, mon-
archs vying for the vast new territories in North America by
sponsoring settlers, from France in the Canadian north, accom-
panied by the apparatus of Frenchness—Jesuits, nuns, French
soldiers, bent on occupying the territory and making Catholics
out of the local Indians. By the beginning of the eighteenth century, they had converted many local tribes and habitants, and
made allies of them in their warlike forays on the English-
speaking Puritans over the border.

In New England when Ranna got there, Protestantism—
Puritanism—was well established; the first settlers had been there
ninety years, since the *Mayflower* landed in 1620. The two groups,
Puritans of English origin and Canadian French, clashed continu-
ously along the borders of Vermont, New Hampshire, and Massachusetts. The violence took the form of savage Indian raids in which
Indian braves, egged on by the French, incited by plunder and religion both, swooped down frequently on the wooden houses of the
stockaded Puritan villages to scalp or kidnap the inhabitants.

A famous raid in 1704 had targeted Deerfield, Massachusetts. French-led Pocumtuc Indians attacked the little settlement
of log houses and stockades, massacred fifty-six of the sleeping
villagers, and kidnapped more than a hundred others as slaves

and chattel, marching them some 350 miles to French-held territories around Montreal. Here the English-speaking Protestant prisoners lived for nearly a decade. Some settled in the French communities and became Catholics, some piously resisted, some of the women—more than you might think—married their Indian captors (strangely, these seem always to have claimed to be Indian chiefs). Eventually, after so many years of leading the free, barefoot life of forest-dwelling Indians instead of the prayer-ridden strictness of their Puritan families, many of the English-speaking kids were reluctant to go home. Some of the "white Indians" never went home, or paid ceremonial visits, trailing their blanket-wearing Indian husbands and dusky, frisky, bead-bedecked offspring behind them.

But the New England communities, passionately concerned for the health and especially the souls of the captured, had been negotiating for the Deerfield captives' release ever since that 1704 raid. They feared that Catholics would try to convert their lost ones, or cause them inadvertently to utter some Papist formula that would send them right to the devil whether they knew it or not. By innocently repeating some phrase from the Catholic rite of baptism, for instance, they might become Papists all unknowingly.

Now it was 1711. In the intervening seven years since the Indian capture of the hundred English-speaking men, women, and children, an exchange deal had been laboriously finalized, a scheme to trade them for French prisoners of the English—usually these were like Ranna, victims taken at sea by the English navy and dropped off in New England, as had happened to the passengers on the ship *Neptune.* Ranna had been captured by a Captain Mathews aboard the *Chester,* and left in New Haven on his own recognizance, as Cousin Emily wrote. The condition of captives such as Ranna was not too terrible; they seemed to be expected to abide by their word not to flee or connive against their captors, whether these were French or English, and mostly they didn't.

Ranna had only a year or so of captivity to endure; in 1713, a group of captured Frenchmen was assembled in Massachusetts to be marched off to Montreal to rejoin their Francophone world. It's here that Ranna Cossitt emerges in the diaries and reports of a Colonel Partridge, the exasperated official in charge of the exchange. Ranna refused to be exchanged.

Partridge writes to Governor Dudley in Montreal of two re‑calcitrant Frenchmen "who will not be p'suaded to go, neither by p'suasions nor force, except they be carried, viz, Cosset & Laffe‑ ver [Le Fevre]. [T]he Capt. hath used all means with them, espe‑ cially Cosset, in so much that I believe if they go into the woods together, they will murder one another before they get to Can‑ ada, Cosset positively refusing to go, Chuseing rather to Remayne a prisoner all his days, as he saith, rather than go with him. The Captaine vehemently mad with him, as he saith, will kill him, & its thought by their violent treatmt one towards another that murder had been done if o' men had not pr'evented itt. They cannot speak together but some fall to blows. . . ."

Partridge adds that they finally "abandon him [Ranna] as a Protestant." C. Alice Baker, author of *True Stories of New England Captives Carried to Canada During the French and Indian Wars*, promises that "the adventures of Cosset and Le Fevre . . . will be narrated later," but, alas, she doesn't do it. We know he stays in Connecticut and gets married. It will be his great‑granddaughter who goes to the Midwest in the 1820s.

10

Anne and God

We know that our forebears were pious in varying degrees, and conventionally churchgoing, with Protestant, often Puritan, backgrounds in a developing country given to religious preoccupations. The evangelical atmosphere of early America informs the tone of a brief memoir by Ranna's great-granddaughter (my great-great-great-grandmother) Anne, the first to have left her recollections in my little cache of ancestral letters. She grew up on the border with Canada, but would be part of the Yankee migration in the 1820s, people taking with them religious enthusiasms and the apparatus of churchgoing as they moved inland from the Eastern Seaboard.

Anne was born in 1779, during the American Revolution, the oldest child in what would be a family of eight children. They lived in Claremont, New Hampshire, and were Anglicans, that is, still part of the Church of England because the Episcopal Church hadn't yet declared itself independent of the English church after the Revolution. It isn't clear that her family was even on the American side in that war; at least one of her uncles, another Ranna, named for his grandfather the first Ranna, in Claremont was a conspicuous Loyalist, or Tory, that is, stuck with the English king, and was confined by his patriotic neighbors to house arrest. This Tory uncle Ranna, born in America, had been ordained in England and was an Anglican minister. He eventually went up to Stanstead, Canada, and made his mark there.

His brother, Anne's father, Ambrose, was referred to as Judge Cossitt, so that was probably his profession, which implies they were at least educated, and possibly relatively prosperous. But Ambrose was not very religious.

His daughter Anne was—she was a serious, naturally pious girl influenced by the religious climate of her childhood, when, despite the moderate Deism of the founders, the Revolution was followed by the so-called Second Great Awakening, a mood of evangelism and religious enthusiasm that swept westward from New York into the Midwest. Whole eastern states were swarming with Methodist and Baptist missionaries and lively camp meetings fraught with sermons, singing, and enthusiastic conversions; one of Anne's brothers became a prominent Presbyterian evangelist. New sects like Mormons and Shakers would arise about now.

You could imagine religion was a comforting response to the anxiety of finding yourself on a dangerous new continent and in the loneliness of the woodsy, isolated settlements. Later people would be afflicted by the advent of science, Darwin and so on, but for late-eighteenth-century America, trust in God was undoubtedly encouraged by the precariousness of existence—He was all you had. And you had the heavy legacy of the Puritans, a legacy ultimately, as V. S. Pritchett put it, one of dullness, though it also had the moral charm of certitude. As religious fervor is back today, we might say it comes and goes like seasonal flu, and each time leaves a nation weakened for the next attack.

Anne was high-strung and susceptible, a pious child drawn to the drama of religion but somewhat embarrassed by her own religious bent in a family not particularly pious. She got her zeal as a child, and though her experience expresses something of the general religious climate in this turbulent period after the American Revolution, the account she left concentrates, rather unfortunately, on her own spiritual progress, when we might have preferred to hear about what she ate or wore. As to the latter, we know the kitchen had no stove in the modern sense, only an open fireplace with a hook built in to hang the pots over the coals, and an adja‑ cent bake oven of brick. Southern families had slaves to tend to the cooking, but New England families usually did not, though they probably had a servant or two.

Still, a lot of the household duties fell on Anne. The dresses of a girl of this period might be either of homespun or of cotton, linen, or wool from one of the newly established mills beginning to be found in New England at this time. If homespun, the cloth was often produced at a spinning bee, where women and girls of a village getting together with their wheels could produce an im‑ pressive amount in a day. A lot of cloth was needed for the Cos‑ sitts, a family of six girls, for their aprons, petticoats, drawers, caps—always white, over dresses of brown or gray, or sprigged with flowers. A lot of sewing and a lot of bending over washtubs.

Whatever she wore, Anne thought surely she was the unluck‑ iest girl in the world, to be born into a family like hers, especially to be the oldest child, having to do all the work for the little ones—Mama always indisposed with another baby on the way— and not a minute even to pray. She had time to read only a chap‑ ter of the Bible in the morning, no one dared tell her she oughtn't to do that, let her sisters jeer and whine as they would: Mary Alma, Elizabeth Ruth, Phoebe, Charlotte, and Lavinia. Surely no one else was burdened with such a mob of clamorous, unreligious little sisters. She was also unlucky in her parents; they were just plain deficient in spirituality: "My father prayed only once or twice a week or on Sunday, and soon once a month and then not at all, indeed there was very little religion in the place." Father would pray over the family at dinnertime, but very short prayers—longer on the Sabbath—and not very sincerely. "Bless this food to thy use and us to thy service, amen."

She thought she would like to pray more often, and took to going out into the garden in the morning, nonchalantly, so they wouldn't know; but even that couldn't last: "Why are you out here? Whom do you expect to see?"

She couldn't pray by her bedside either; Lavinia and Phoebe were sleeping, or, if awake, noisy and laughing. She thought a person ought to pray two or three times a day but it was hope· less at home. Maybe she would leave it till she was older. She reasoned that she wasn't so bad—the deacon and the priest told idle stories and played in plays, danced and sang nonsensical songs. "I am no worse than they be," she said to herself. Maybe she wouldn't go straight to hell if she backslid a little.

She had a pretty voice, and her parents had sent her to singing school. She liked plays and dancing, and she liked singing, and people liked to hear her sing. She knew she sang well but she wasn't sure it was all right to be proud of it. But didn't her voice come from God?

And another theological question weighed on her: even if you danced and sang, and played in plays, you couldn't really know if you were damned or saved. Some people said it was already de· cided. The Baptists said that. The Baptist preachers had meetings and sometimes she stole away to hear them. These Calvinists were not people her family associated with, but they were good people, everyone said, and Calvinists thought it was already decided when you were born, and nothing you did could change whether you were saved or damned.

"That makes no sense," her father argued. "If it be already decided, you might as well do as you please, even if it pleases you to be bad."

Salvation by faith or by works. That was all people talked about: could you reverse a possibly adverse cosmic judgment if God hath decided against you? She thought about this a lot and couldn't help herself from praying (silently) that being good could just nudge the balance in your favor, in case you were teetering on the brink. When she was fifteen, her father invited a Methodist preacher to come preach at their house. The whole community came to hear—some people even brought their servants. It seemed to her that what the man said made sense: to be saved you had three paths—to have faith, and be good, and do good works. Though it was frightening to think you might go to hell, it was wonderful to think you could avoid it if you believed, avoided sin, and became a Methodist. The Methodist preacher was young, and didn't turn away the questions of women or girls like her who wanted to learn more. Some churches dismissed women unless they sinned, and then turned on them the way the Massachusetts people had turned on the girls in Salem.

Father and Mother, having invited the Methodist preacher in an ecumenical spirit, were not so sure about him: "they said he tried to make out the Methodists right and no other"—but Anne takes some of their message to heart: "I didn't want my name to be cast out as evil so I thought I would not commit any more sins than I could help." How modern was her mood of intermittent resolution—like people today with their dieting. Trying not to commit any more sins than she could help, she continued in a high state of religious anxiety through her teenage years, always thinking herself eternally damned. Sometimes the devil told her the Lord wouldn't accept such weak, feeble prayers as someone like her could make—"I must use the form that some grate larnt person had made." She tried to copy out prayers from the books of prayers and sermons, but they seemed empty, and then her heart would spill over with her own words—"I would brake out of the form and pray to the Lord for such things as I felt in my soul I needed and the Lord would bless me. . . ."

She liked to read writings like those of Jonathan Edwards, whose scary warnings gave her thrilling torments: "It is to be as·cribed to nothing else, that you did not go to hell the last night—that you were suffered to awake again in this world, and yet . . . it is nothing but his hand that holds you from falling into the fire every moment"—words definitely calculated to frighten impres·sionable young girls. Papa's grandma had been at Salem, where all those troubles were, a hundred years before.

But Anne couldn't really concentrate on being good all the time—she had gentlemen callers, and work to do around the house—with so many siblings there was so much to see to; and there were parties! People would come to the house to hear preaching and music. We notice that these Cossitts weren't troubled with Puritan compunctions about dancing and singing and possibly drink.

She was eighteen. She felt her conviction wearing off, but it was more put aside than forgotten, and she still tried not to com·mit sin, but shun it as much as possible and bring herself to reckoning every night. "I drew up a resolution to bring myself to strict account every night and without partiality think over all my good and bad deeds. I often grieved to think my bad deeds were so many more than the good." She ended by deciding that maybe she should wait till she was settled in the world before worrying about the state of her soul.

As seems to have happened to everyone whose religious tes-
timonials at this period have come down to us, one wonderful
day she knew she was saved. She had never been so happy!
"There is heaven in my soul, the earth is beneath, the moon is
under my feet, I feel my soul all peace, joy and love to God. Am
I awake or is it a dream? No, I am not deluded. He has forgiven
my sins and filled my soul with love!"

Whatever she was reading, her account of her religious torment
pretty much follows the form of the devotional literature of the
period, with its sense of sin, despair, and, finally, joyous discovery
of God's forgiveness. There were people she knew who read the
frivolous gothic novels, works like *The Mysteries of Udolpho,* or
Vathek, or any of the first works by the promising Anglo-Irish
writer Maria Edgeworth, or the American gothic novel *Wieland*
by Charles Brockden Brown, which came out in 1798—in fact
there is no echo of any imaginative literature in her (or her daughter's) memoirs except the Bible and maybe *Pilgrim's Progress.* Luckily for her longing to be settled in the world, she had a special
admirer about now, 1798: Mr. John Perkins, a young man whose
religious attitude she admired and whom she thought suitably pious: "By his conversation I thought he knew more of religion than
I did and I thought he would be my help in the way of the Soul."

She doesn't say how they got to know each other. A lot of the
social activity of the community seemed to center on a church,
as it had for the Puritan forefathers.

The wedding was a simple affair. She was eighteen when she
married Mr. Perkins, and religion continued to be a main feature of their social life, as it must have been throughout the region. She expected happiness.

11

Huts

The newly wed Perkinses, Anne and John, homesteaded near the recently settled Lake Memphrémagog, in what was then called Lower Canada. Lake Memphrémagog was a very large, cold lake in a bitter climate, dividing Quebec and Vermont for forty miles of the border, and had attracted a few Loyalist families fleeing the American Revolution. The couple built a little hut of a house, and farmed three acres of corn, beans, potatoes, and cucumbers. The house was probably of log, and small.

Near Norris, Tennessee, there's an outdoor museum run by the Smithsonian, several acres of reconstructed early cabins our fore-fathers lived in, original structures carefully moved onto the site for preservation. Such huts were very often daily reality for people at the end of the eighteenth century; until they could build better, they had to live in simple huts or cabins, such as Anne was living in when she went into labor in winter and her husband had gone off to find help. Preserved in Tennessee is the actual cabin of Mark Twain's family, dating from the 1830s. It's aston-ishing to consider how many iconic American figures lived in similar cabins, buildings startling in their primitive simplicity, often dirt-floored, with open fireplaces, the log walls chinked with mud. Anne and John Perkins, and later their daughter Cath-arine and her young doctor husband, all lived in huts or cabins at some point. The rustic life my parents emulated in summers in Michigan, similarly near the Canadian border, was based on this tradition—summer cabin life grew out of the folk memory of life in such cabins not so far back.

Anne wrote about her lonely cabin life on the border with Canada. Besides succumbing to the religious fervor common at the time, the young couple had real life troubles. They lived a mile away from any neighbors, and they found their neighbors a cheating lot.

"We met with many disappointments, the property we carried to Canada we had trusted out and we could not collect it again. And though we had by our provisions kept three families from starving, they would not pay us one farthing. That year was the scarcest I ever saw for provisions; many families lived entirely upon wild onions for several weeks. . . ."

She doesn't like her neighbors: "a dreadful loose sect of people. Their general character was lying, swearing, stealing, mischief making, Sabbath breaking and getting drunk. O! How I felt, but nonetheless there was some well disposed people there. . . . One Sunday several of them—the wicked—came to see me. I entertained them by reading the scriptures to them and they never came to see me again."

We don't know how she defined wickedness or knew it in her visitors, but can imagine a bunch of jolly, kindly, bonneted onion eaters bringing cakes to the poor Perkins wife whose husband was never at home, only to have a very dull time on their visit.

Conrad Richter was the great novelist of subsistence life on the frontier, and he makes it sound even worse than Anne does: Indian attacks, drafty cabins with buckskin doors, well water, fever, death. Looking back on it later, Anne remembered one particularly hard time, in the wilds in the winter of 1800, when

she went into labor. This is her second baby; she's now twenty·
one years old:

> On the 19th of October at evening I was taken ill. My hus·
> band immediately sent a man for the doctor who lived ten
> miles off. I remained all night in the most racking pain.
> Morning came and no help came to my assistance. Some
> women stood around and said "She will die for there is no
> help." I was the only one that believed I was not dangerous.
> However, I was delivered before twelve o'clock of a daughter.
> The child was well but I was brought so low that my life was
> despaired of. I suffered much for want of good care but my
> husband did everything in his power for me.

The baby she refers to is Catharine, born up there in the woods,
with the neighbors shaking their heads over Anne's state, bound to
die. One conclusion to take from this, at least, is that midwesterners
come of stalwart stock. She was laid low by this last baby:

> When my babe was five weeks old my husband thought it
> best to carry me to the Doctor's to stay while he repaired
> his sleigh, got his horse that was thirty miles off and made
> ready to go to Claremont in New Hampshire where my
> parents lived. My husband carried my children down to the
> lake, and then carried me. We got into a canoe and went
> two miles breaking the ice before the canoe, for the water
> was freezing. We went to a house to stay that night, expect·
> ing to go in a sleigh to the Doctor's but there came a
> storm of snow and wind that night so it was thought best for
> me to stay there while Mr. Perkins went after his sleigh
> and horse.

After he was gone, I was taken so ill that all around me thought I was dying. They sent for the Doctor. When he came, they told him they believed that I would not go out of that house till I was carried out a corpse. They thought my senses were so gone that I knew nothing that was said. But I knew all that was said.

However, she doesn't die, but slowly recuperates, and they continue their journey of nearly two weeks and arrive in Claremont, where her father and mother—Ambrose and Anne Cole Cossitt—live, and where she had grown up. Anne is still very ill and doesn't feel up to much until the following May. In June they retrace their journey of 140 miles to their farm near Canadian Lake Memphrémagog.

Here were many trials and afflictions. I was often left alone for more than a week at a time. Some times I suffered much with fear.

There are wind in the trees, bears in the corn, smallpox in the offing, and possibly unfriendly Indians. She is consoled by her religion, but her physical situation does not improve for another year, when a proper house is built, another family comes to live with them, and someone repays a debt of $150.

To collect it, Mr. Perkins, as she refers to him, "had to go thirty miles through the woods, no house in all the way." Once he is caught shelterless in a storm, has to spend the night in freezing rain under a blanket of bark and boughs, falls ill when he arrives at the rendezvous, and lies ill for several weeks, so that in all he is gone more than ten weeks, during which time Anne has no news of him.

When he had been gone eight weeks, I found my provisions were growing short and I must do something about getting more. I went two miles thru the woods to a place where I thought I could get what I wanted. When I got there, I found I must go one mile farther. I bought what pork I thought would do me two months and made calculations for some grain to be ground and brought to me, then returned home much fatigued, gave my children their supper and put them to bed. I then sat down in great distress of mind. . . . I feared he had perished in the woods, he had been gone so much longer than I expected, I was sure he was dead.

She bucks herself up with the thought that she must live for her children. Here, alas, her manuscript breaks off.

Twenty·six years later, the baby, Catharine, is grown up and marries a young doctor, with whom she travels to rural Ohio, where they find things not much better, and she too will start out married life in a hut.

The French philosopher Gaston Bachelard writes about a hut dream, which he says is common to everybody, a dream of ideal coziness and safety. I wonder, though, about the mean little hut that's your only recourse, like Anne's: did it seem cozy and safe? Bachelard's idea is that you are snug within a small dwelling set on the edge of a wilderness, warmed by a fire, protected from a scene of wild nature outside.

Unlike most of us (in Bachelard's view), neither Catharine nor Anne were drawn to huts. I am, myself. My own first hut, my for·mative hut, was my father's duck blind, a chilly shack by the Rock River, roofed with leaves, walled with rushes, water lapping under the floor, hideously cold. There my father and his friends would crouch for hours, smelling of wool and gunpowder (and Four Roses), while I, bundled as stiffly as a papoose on a board, solemnly minded the warnings that here you had to be as still and wary as any wild creature. It was thrilling when the ducks and geese mistook us for an innocent clump of rushes and came flapping and calling toward us, and I don't remember much concern for their fate, though later in the year, I felt anguished for rabbits and squirrels hanging in the garage, hated their gamy smell. And have grown up to scorn hunting.

In the duck blind there was nothing to do but gape at the capricious river, which might bring anything floating along, admiring the beauty of the brown, frosted banks, and the hoar-rimed twigs and rushes, and winter birds in the bare trees.

In France, we have a hut, a little stone building that gazes out at the Seine River. Of course it has running water and lights, but still, it gives the dweller some idea about living in a hut long-term, a spiritual discipline, possibly not much fun.

12

1800

On the day Anne Perkins gave birth to her second child, Catharine Anne, in October 1800, John Adams was president of the new republic. Voting for the next president had begun the April before, and was still going on, though the results wouldn't be known until early 1801—it would be Thomas Jefferson. Though the mention of Jefferson evokes Paris, powdered wigs, and frock coats, farmers like John and Anne Perkins were not so elegantly dressed; John would have worn short breeches and three-cornered hats, and shoes with buckles, still much like the costumes we think of the Pilgrims wearing. The dress of a farmer's wife was still simple homespun linen or cotton, darkish in color for day, with an apron, perhaps a fichu, and a cap or bonnet. All the ladies in daguerreotypes taken around then (necessarily after 1839) are wearing some kind of head covering, as was Anne's daughter Catharine when she was painted in 1849, as shown in the front matter.

In Europe, though Anne and John Perkins were perhaps not aware of it, the French Revolution had come to an end, and the Napoleonic Wars were just beginning; the year 1800 would see the Battle of Marengo and the looting of Egypt, events they probably heard nothing of. America had long been at quasi war with France and Britain, but was signing a treaty ending it. Smallpox vaccination was beginning in America, but Anne doesn't refer to it, and when the disease breaks out in their district, they expect to get it, though they quarantine themselves and do not. (When her daughter Catharine later lost three of her little children in a week, it was to scarlet fever.) Anne barely mentions any world events, and probably didn't hear of them, given the difficulty of having news; for example, news of her husband from thirty miles away. If they had worries about Indian raids by 1800, she doesn't mention them either, but they might well have, as this warfare continued for decades, well into the 1830s.

Anne had enough to worry about without world affairs too: where was Mr. Perkins, and what had kept him away without sending news of himself to his stranded wife? He did indeed al- most catch his death on his trip through the woods—from mumps—and was nearly six weeks convalescing. We can piece something of young Perkins's journeys from letters to his father-in-law, the practical Ambrose Cossitt, for whom he was apparently acting in a land deal of some kind, or owed money to, apologizing for his long absence.

It appears that Cossitt had sent him somewhere to make good a legal matter. Collecting a debt could be a tricky business in those rough-and-ready days, apparently, sometimes hinging on dashing to the courthouse before someone else did. When John Perkins arrives in Canada, he finds that some mysterious chicanery is afoot that involves racing creditors to Quebec to pay a debt before they could enforce some condition.

"I set out from this town on foot. . . . They had one day's start of me but I traveled as far in two days as they did in three.

"Then at Three Rivers I took Post Stage and went past them in the road, they not knowing me. I went & took out Melborn [Melbourne] Charter & got a coppy before they came into town and completely saved the land, so that you may tell Judge Kings- bury that the business is done to his mind."

During his absence the roof of his house had fallen in, though there was no damage; Anne and the children had been staying with her parents, to whom he is writing. He adds that "to my greatest satisfaction I found [proved] that I had not ran away as many said."

Had he been thought to be someone who ran out on debts?

A letter from Ambrose Cossitt, 1804

13

John Perkins Too Sees God

Anne Perkins, smitten with excessive piety in her adolescence, now seems content to leave the family's spiritual condition to her young husband. In 1812, he has a religious revelation, and his account, like hers, contains the conventional ingredients, especially a catatonic state and a vivid dream, the whole thing harrowing and shattering to his state of mind and his metaphysical condition. Was it a bad dream? Or possibly even a seizure? We see by his language that he has read the Book of Revelation and John Bunyan:

TESTIMONY, AUGUST 12, 1812, BY JOHN A. PERKINS

The last week in August of 1812 I, well in my right mind though in great trouble for ten days [about] what I should do to be saved and as I had felt my sins forgiven on the night before I went to bed in my right mind, resigned to the will of God with a determination to live a religious life all my days [even] if I never was made sure of the new birth in the Kingdom of Christ; but while I was meditating on the goodness of God, then came a shock that struck me motionless.

While my senses were greater than ever before as I was made sensible that the Lord was about to show me of things that are to be in the future of all I ever desired to see, those things what I once disbelieved but now I know to my satisfaction. . . .

I settled one question in my mind: faith without works are in vain, for any to expect to be saved if they die in their sins for this is contrary to the words of our Saviour.

I was taken through the heavens by a devil on the one hand and the Glory on the other. . . .

He was taken on a Miltonian or Dante-esque tour, seeing galaxies, multitudes, glorious choruses, a scary vision of the Day of Judgment, and a glimpse of future punishment. "While I was in this dreaming or catatonic state I couldn't move my limbs. Anne came into the room but couldn't see what I saw. I wrote it down so that my children's children's children may know that forever has no end."

His handwriting is large and forthright, with a terrific flourish over the *P* in Perkins; but neither his panache nor his religion was to avail him, for he died young. After he falls ill, about this time, they receive a little letter from her mother, suggesting a remedy for his ailment.

Claremont June 21, 1814

Dear Children

I received a letter from Anne last week which says Mr. Perkins is very unwell, likewise Mr. Willard Mack was here and says Mr. Perkins is confined with rheumatism. I have lately heard of a new medison by a Friend.

Bathe him in Pork brine with a flannel cloth three quarters of an hour three nights going. Take a little saffron to guard his stomach. It has done great cures.

I have lately received a letter from Franceway that he and Mary are coming home in September if [it] be possible. I will come and make you a visit when they come.

We are all well. This from your Affectionate Mother

Anne C. Cossit

Franceway is one of Anne's brothers, named for the original François, Ranna's brother. Naturally pork brine didn't do much good in curing a cancer, and poor young Mr. Perkins died in 1814, before he was forty.

To finish with Anne's story, after John Perkins's death in 1814, she marries a cheerful-sounding person named Meyrick or Mirick, but, though not yet forty herself, has no further children. They move to the Midwest a little while after her daughter Catharine marries in 1827.

14

Some Stories from the Life of Catharine Perkins

The lives of people long ago are so unlike and so like ours. The questions they raise for us are abiding: How did Anne and John Perkins meet? How did their daughter Catharine meet her husband, Eleazer? We have no idea what on earth those young girls, Anne Cossitt or her daughter Catharine, knew about sex before they were married. We do know from Catharine something about the courtship anxieties of maidens of long ago.

She was the one born in the winter wilderness in 1800; and much of my impression of what life was like for the first midwestern settlers comes from her memoir. Catharine and Eleazer Martin's history gives another vivid glimpse of how harsh midwestern life was at this early period, nearly two hundred years ago, and if her memory had softened some things by the time she sat down to write in 1876, she had saved letters from her girlhood that give a lively sense of what she went through—letters especially revealing about what life and marriage customs were for a young American woman on the frontier in the early nineteenth century, so much more difficult than, say, the lives of the English Austen girls, who were more or less her contemporaries, though Catharine had probably never heard of them.

It was Catharine who went with her new husband to the Midwest in 1827 in the vast Yankee migration of those years. To be sure, there were already people living in that region—French-Indian families, Native American villages—which had been populated by the latter for a thousand years. But Europeans were few, just some trappers, farmers, and missionaries who came as early as the end of the seventeenth century, and the forlorn French girls sent out to be mates. Indian raids were not entirely over, and until well into the nineteenth century there was a serious danger of being scalped. The brutality and capriciousness of the Indian wars, at least according to the great historian Francis Parkman, is now hard to believe, and the absence of references to them in these memoirs suggests they had been so thoroughly accepted as a part of life as to not need mention, or else that the dangers had died down by then, even though the great battles like Little Bighorn and Wounded Knee lay far in the future.

Catharine writes about a happy childhood spent between Stanstead in Canada with her grandparents and, because her parents, Anne and John Perkins, lived in that hut in the woods, being sent to board with various relatives in towns in Vermont and New Hampshire. People seem to have lived very often with their relatives or even neighbors in order to go to a certain school or to teach, or merely to help with some winter or summer tasks—in the case of young women, sewing bonnets or making dresses and quilts.

> In those days Lower Canada was a perfect wilderness, as well as the Northern States of New England being a wooded country . . . and it must have required very hard work to the first settlers to cut down the timber to make as good farms as there were when I got to be a woman, though they had schools and tried to educate their children as well as all New England did, but were behind New England in high schools and academies.

My parents took much pains to give me and my brother (who was older than I was) all the advantages of an education that they could. I remember they hired me boarded in other districts where they had better teachers. Especially in the Marlow neighborhood, as they called it. And I remember being in Unity and Claremont [two towns in New Hampshire] with my grandparents when I was 8 or 9 for more than two years.

Her Perkins grandparents lived in Unity. It was her mother's father, Ambrose Cossitt, the religious skeptic, who lived in Claremont and died in 1809:

I remember it with vivid recollection, as he was the first person I ever saw die. I remember, a few days before he died, a lawyer came there to write his will, and as I heard them talking about it, in another room, I asked what Grandpa was going to will me, and Uncle Ambrose Jr. said he was going to will me an old cat. Then I went off crying, as I was not very fond of cats, nor am not to this day.

A few years later, in 1814 when she's fourteen, she will lose her father, John Perkins, whom pork brine could not save.

That summer, before my school was finished, my mother sent for me to come home. My father was very sick with canser, of which he died in August. My dear father, he had been a professed Christian for several years, and he was glad to go, and he was with Jesus. His sufferings were dreadful. My dear mother was left a lone widow, as I am now. He left a small farm with a comfortable house and barn, and we lived near what was then called the Bebee [Beebe] Plain. I went back and finished my school, and came home and stayed through the winter.

Unmarried young women even from educated families had to get their livings or contribute in some way, as we learn from the fiction of the period. As soon as Catharine finished her own education, whatever it consisted of, at about age sixteen she began doing one of the few things a well-brought-up girl could do—teach school, which was held during the summer months:

> In 1825 through the summer I taught in Stanstead, where I had the summer before. I was boarding at a Mr. Batchel-ders, a short half-mile from the school-house.

Another time:

> I was teaching school there, and boarding at Esq. Enock Burnhams . . . in those days ladies did not teach much in the winter, on account of the deep snows and cold.

Weather permitting, she slogged off every day along muddy roads to little schoolhouses in rural Canada, and she talks of boarding a number of times with other families in order to teach nearby. It's hard to imagine the level of education purveyed by a sixteen-year-old—surely not very high. It's revealing that things change very slowly; my father, in rural Iowa at the end of the same century, also taught in the one-room school where he had been a pupil, when he was old enough to replace the teacher—at the age of fifteen. He wrote:

> In those days [around 1900], country one-room schools consisted of three plateaus of academic work, namely A, B and C, the latter being beginners, or grade one. By the time I was eleven or twelve I had been through the work two or three

times, and finally in desperation, when I was about fifteen, I assumed the role of teacher, much to the discomfort of said teacher.

He describes the fate of other teachers in the area; one unlucky fellow over in Hacklebarney, where the locals especially scorned any education beyond the three Rs, was chased down the road with bullets pinging at his heels, fired from the .22s the kids would take to school. "To carry a gun to school was the accepted thing—in fact I had done so when I was going to Shunem, not to run the teacher out but to bag an unsuspecting rabbit."

A side note: Hacklebarney is still described as an unmapped area of southeastern Iowa, which maybe explains a lot about the distinctive Iowan politics.

Just to keep track, Catharine was the great-great-granddaughter of the first Ranna Cossitt. When she says that ladies didn't teach in winter, she seems to mean by "lady" a social distinction, not just female. We can see her concern for propriety in her earnest little essay "Refinement," written about now, testimony to a seventeen-year-old's dream of a comfortable and elegant life, though we can't guess where a girl born in a hut in the Canadian woods would have gotten such aspirations:

REFINEMENT BY CATHARINE ANNE PERKINS

Some look with envious eye upon the virtues of another, and, as if they obscured their own reputation, do all they can to cast a cloud over their bright shinings, that theirs may appear more conspicuous. Would this so frequently appear did all possess a refined and virtuous education?

No. How quiet and pleasing would be the effect. One would, by admiring and imitating the virtues, promoting the happiness, and spreading the fame of another, reflect a borrowed splendor on their own merits and make them really greater. While one seemed solicitous only for the happiness of another, oneself would be happy and beloved. Ladies who had merit improved by refinement would possess in the decline of life, an influence more flattering over their acquaintance and even over the men, than their beauty did in youth over their admirers. And those gentlemen who at present often degrade themselves into fops and coxcombs to please the ladies, would discover that their esteem is not to be gained but by exerting the most manly and virtuous talents in every public and private station. Mutual esteem would produce urbanity. And a mutual desire to please would give affability to manners, and delicacy to sentiment. Both sexes, instead of corrupting each other by vicious principles and immoral conduct would become rivals in the cause of virtue, and thus, promote both public good and private happiness.

Stanstead Nov. 5, 1817

15

The Story of Catharine Continued

Now, 1817, and for the next few years, Catharine's life consists of moving from teaching post to teaching post, and from one relative to another.

> The next spring, in 1817, I commenced school teaching, in Derby, Vermont. It was a country place & I boarded a good deal at Esq. Weight's. Mrs. W. was a dear, sweet woman—I loved her very much, and she was every inch a lady. She had two sons at home then, but they afterwards came to this state [Illinois], Jacksonville, I believe, where Charles, the oldest one, died. Erastus, I heard of him as living in Springfield, a few years ago.

What wonderful names people had back then: Erastus, Ambrose, Franceway, Eleazer. How often they died young. And how industriously Catharine worked at her compositions and dreamed of her future. Meantime, there was some social life, and many long, boring evenings by the fireside with needlework. A dance or church event would be looked forward to with an intensity we can only imagine. It is this year, 1817, that she meets her future husband, but she doesn't marry for ten more years; the course of love is far from smooth, and will bring her grief—endless pregnancies and nine children, eight of whom she will see die.

Writing at age seventy-six, Catharine is able to remember

clearly the ups and downs, intermittent pains, and charms of her courtship by Eleazer Martin, especially how it began:

> I was boarding at Esq. Davenport's, near his brother's, the first time he called to see me and asked me if he might spend the evening? I was so bashful and scared I thought I would not have him stop for anything, then or ever, but did not like to tell him no, right out, so I told him I did not wish to have company that evening, and meant the answer for always, but he did not take it so, but said he would call the next Sunday evening, but seeing I had got caught by trying to soften my refusal, I said, very well and bowed him out. And when I came to talk with Mrs. Davenport, she thought so high of him, I was glad I did make the mistake in my bashfulness and confusion.

16

The Inappropriate Letter

We have to assume that Catharine was pretty, like all young women in stories. At one point, her situation was a little like an early-nineteenth-century novel: more or less alone in the world, she receives mash notes from a married man, and wonders what to do, and gets misunderstood as a hussy. *Ma vie est un roman!* say the French.

A pretty, vulnerable young woman boarder could inadvertently make trouble in a household even in those primmer times, and it seems that Anne, Catharine's mother, was no more watchful than was Mrs. Bennet—Anne's far more worldly English counterpart—when it came to Lydia and Kitty. With Anne preoccupied with her new husband, Catharine was a bit forlorn and unprotected, more like Jane Eyre than like the comfortable daughters of Rev. Austen, though the Austen girls and those in Austen's novels too were equally mindful of their fragile economic situations and marriage prospects. Catharine would have found their stories reassuring, but she didn't read them. (*Pride and Prejudice* was not published in the United States until 1832.) In fact Catharine didn't approve of novel reading, at least when she was very young; perhaps she had gotten some of her hopes from books and been disappointed. Her experience had begun to teach her that there was no point in indulging dreams of ease and romance:

On Novel Reading by Catharine Anne Perkins

Jan 2nd 1818

What is more detrimental to the happiness of young people than novel reading? It is like a worm at the root of a tender plant, it raises and sinks the mind to extremes, which is unpleasant to the possessor and troublesome to others whose nerves are not so peculiarly fine. It gives a romantic imagination and an affected air and leaves in the mind a gloomy void which nothing but the false scenes of imagination can occupy or a length of time dissipate. It gives imaginary felicity which cannot be realized and distaste of the sober scenes of real life. . . .

That Catharine should recall the episode of the improper letter sixty years later suggests how unprotected she felt herself to be and was. As she tells it, she had boarded during one teaching season with a Davenport family, whom she had liked. Later, she was living with her grandmother, probably her Cossitt grandmother, Anne Cole, and Mary Alma, one of her unmarried aunts, in the house of another Cossitt uncle, probably Samuel:

Some time in the winter I had, according to promises, written to Mrs. D[avenport], and in the spring I received an answer from her, written by her husband, as I suppose she was out of the habit of writing much, as she had a family of small children. My aunt Mary was gone when I received the letter and I was sitting in my uncle's room with his wife, and she asked me to read it to her, so I opened it and read it aloud.

But there was another letter folded and done up by itself, inside, though not sealed, that I did not read, for I was a little surprised and did not know who it could be from. So I waited until I went into our rooms and then read it, and to my great astonishment, it was from the same gentleman who wrote the other, only without his wife's knowing it. It was only a friendly letter, no love in it—and at the end, as he was excusing himself for writing without his wife's knowl, edge, he said he was not disposed to affect, nor did he possess an unholy desire towards any woman.

I felt very much insulted, and tried to make myself be, lieve he was drunk when he wrote it, but there was the writ, ing, plain and nice, as in the other letter. When aunt Mary came home, I showed it to her and asked her advise. Asked if I should not send it back to him without any answer. After considering on it, she said it might fall into other hands than his and make trouble, and thought it best to take no notice of it and never answer either of the letters. So I took her ad, vise and never did answer either of them.

But my trouble with that letter was not over yet. I had hid it away among my grandma's things, so no one I thought would find it. I knew that my uncle's wife was a meddlesome woman, always prying into other people's affairs, with which she had no rightful concern. Sure enough, she had noticed my not reading the inside letter, and when we happened to be all out of our rooms, she had found it and read it. Whether she showed it to my uncle I do not remember, but I would have preferred he should see it, for if she told him, she would make it worse than it was.

Some days after, my uncle came in while I was in their room, pulled off his hat, sat it on a chair to do something the other side of the room, and as I passed by it I saw a letter di, rected to my mother. I catched it out and said what are you writing to my mother, I want to see it. He sprang towards me and tried to catch the letter from me. I would not let him

have it until he read it [aloud] and then I knew his wife's
meanness. He had made a "mountain of a mole hill," about
that letter and advised my mother to come right down and
take me home, for fear what might happen. While I was as
innocent as an infant of having given him any excuse for writing it.

My uncle said I had kept a secret and would not read it to
them. I told him I did not consider that I was under his or his
wife's care, that I was with my aunt Mary and that I read the
letter to her and asked her advise. He hardly believed me,
but my aunt, coming in just then, told him I had told her and
she advised me to take no notice of it, and I had never answered either of them letters "as the least said was the soonest
mended." So the letter to my mother was torn up. I had another good cry over the affair and that was the end of it, except in my mind, as young people feel very sensitive about
such things.

17

Catharine's Romance

From 1819 to 1822 Catharine's incipient romance continues with young Dr. Martin. They would not be married until she was twenty-six, just about the average age, or a trifle older, for a bride at this period; marriage age had been slowly rising since the mid-1700s. "I think it was the first or the second week of school that my aunt's little boy came up laughing to tell me that the afternoon before, Dr. Martin had called and inquired for me."

Dr. Martin asks to walk her home, they begin seeing each other over the school term, and by the time she is to leave in the fall, they are engaged: "We had agreed before this to spend our lives together, whenever he got into business so he could afford to marry."

With that they seem to go their separate ways for several years. Their correspondence is at first circumspect, and Eleazer is evasive, in no hurry to marry, and sounds rather caddish sometimes, with his various excuses for not setting a date:

> I loved you and could not think of reducing you to poverty by marrying you without the prospect of even a competency.
>
> Yet Catharine if you ever did believe me when I spoke or wrote, . . . Oh! If you ever placed implicit confidence in what I told you believe me now this once and I will tell you all. . . .
>
> Believe me I am still the same unchanged in Heart if my conduct varied; yes, Catharine I still love you as sincerely as I ever did & I can boldly say never made a protestation of love to you that was not dictated by my heart;

but I am a wounded spirit, and it was this that forced me from you and has since prevented me from writing to you. The pride of my heart was sufficient to over come my love. . . .

So it goes for another three pages of close-written protestations. He sticks to his story of not being able to afford to marry.

For a time Catharine hadn't been really sure she was engaged at all, and when she had other offers, she hardly knew what to say. Her heart had been set on him.

18

The Affair of the Locket

Aunts, uncles, cousins—Catharine had them in droves. The problems and perils for an unmarried young woman in her midtwenties making her own way were much more serious in 1823 than they would be today, and you can read between the lines that her various aunts and uncles were saying to themselves, "What is to happen to Catharine?" Their concern about this can be inferred from the affair of the locket. Her uncles urge her to marry someone she doesn't love—the widower of her favorite aunt, Charlotte, a Mr. Voorhies, a scoundrel, as it turns out.

Catharine had foreseen her aunt's death in a dream:

> Some people say that coming events cast their shadows before them, and I am inclined to think they do, for several times in my life I have seemed to have a presentiment and dreams that seemed to identify events that I knew nothing of till years afterward, tho the one I shall relate now came soon afterward.
>
> The next summer, I think in 1823, I was teaching in Esq. Rose's district through the summer, and in the fall was sewing several weeks at Dr. Whitchers, an old friend, and all at once I was thinking of my dear aunt Charlotte, as being dead, and that she wanted me to take care of her little son Augustus, and no one knew how distressed I felt.

Later she has another premonitory dream, one that gives the only hint that she might have read some novels; perhaps, by the

time she came to write her memoir, she had read (despite its reputation for coarseness) *Jane Eyre,* a work that uses several highly
symbolic dreams with some of the same imagery. In the second
dream, Catharine is in a field surrounded by cheerful little trees
"coming out of the same root," but they are swept away by a wind-
storm, causing her to weep in anguish. Then six other sprouts appear, "just as pretty as those that were gone," but these are
destroyed too. "My distress was so great that I could not get rid of
it." This dream seems to foretell the deaths of the children she
would eventually bear, and that is her interpretation when she
looks back on it in 1876.

She comments, "Some might think this dream is made up to
fit the occasion, but it is not, as I am a Christian woman. I dreamed
it nearly two years before I was married and could never forget it."
Of course it came true:

> A few months afterwards I had a letter from her husband,
> saying that my dear aunt was no more. I, of course, answered
> his letter and he kept on writing several, and I answered
> them, as he was a splendid letter writer, but no love in them,
> only friendship.
>
> In the spring of 1824, Dr. Martin came up the second
> time (I think) to see me, and said he should leave Strafford,
> and when he went home, he went to Georgeville, a little village
> in Stanstead, near the lake, what was once called Copp's Ferry,
> but did not like it and went to Williamstown for a month or
> two, as his father was laid up and needed him.
>
> When he was at our house I told him of my aunt's death
> and very innocently showed him the letters her husband had
> written to me, as I thought of them only as from a friend.

I'm not sure I believe her about this. It seems as if her unconscious motivation was to make Eleazer jealous. She then adds a
curious detail about portrait painting:

> Pictures and likenesses were scarce in those days, but the fall
> before, there had been a celebrated artist from Montreal and
> I got my likeness taken on Ivory, to put in a large locket.
> Those who were accustomed to looking at likenesses, thought
> it a very good one. I showed it to Dr. Martin, for whom I had
> expressly got it painted. His not being much accustomed to
> painting, and my being present with it, he did not think it
> very good. Looked at it and laid it down and never asked me
> for it.

Apparently looking at pictures was a sort of skill or training,
not usual in their daily lives at this time.

> He told me years after, that after he left me, he was so sorry
> that he did not take it. As for the letters, he had more insight
> into them than I did, for he was sure the gentleman meant to
> propose marriage, which he did, not long afterwards. The Dr.
> thought it was not right for me to keep me waiting and nei-
> ther marry me nor let me marry anybody else, if I wished to,
> so he concluded he would start west and go as far as [New]
> York State and find a place to practice.

In low spirits, Eleazer sets out on horseback, traveling west in
search of a medical practice:

> In NY I was disappointed by not being able to find an eligi-
> ble place to locate myself and notwithstanding spent several

months riding through different parts of the state. I once thought myself settled and entered into a verbal contract of partnership with a Physician near Rochester NY but he was too much like me in [being] subject to depression of spirits & he began to fear there would not be sufficient business for both, and I therefore left him; he is now however very urgent in soliciting my return. . . .

Starting up as a doctor seems not to have been easy in the best of circumstances, and it will turn out that Eleazer was what we would now think of as bipolar. He tries for a while with a Dr. Gregory in New York and then moves on to Ohio, where he begins to practice, then falls ill with "billious fever." Ohio at this time, the 1820s, was very much the frontier. He doesn't write to Catharine for another year.

But I will go back to my own life [writes Catharine], which was a very sad one, though I tried to keep it from the world.
Soon after Dr. Martin visited me in N.Y., Mr. V[oorhies] did propose marriage to me, and my uncle F[ranceway] K. Cossitt also urging me to marry him. But no, my heart belonged to another, and I could not and would not. I told him [Mr. Voorhies] that I meant nothing but friendship, and love for my dear aunt, for I had long been engaged to another—a Dr. M.—but to soften my refusal a little, I sent him my miniature, which the Dr. seemed to care so little about.

The disappointed Voorhies, the widower of her aunt Charlotte, vows to treasure the miniature. He was a clever letter writer, with lots of homilies and classical references, and was the only person of a literary turn in her correspondence, despite misspelling Addison: "It is a well-known saying of Mr. Adison that it is impossible for a man to be idle and innocent. There are some hours of the day I am entirely at a loss how to dispose of after having gone through the toils of the day, and then become satiated with reading and finally distracted with one's own thoughts, which are more rapid than the lightning's glance—it becomes a source of relief to write, for then the vagaries of the mind are fettered. . . ."

Catharine writes: "I never heard of Mr. Voorhies after, except through my uncles once or twice, till about the winding up of the rebellion, one of the last battles, I think, on the Mississippi. I saw an account of a Colonel Voorhies of Tennessee and his whole regiment being taken by the Union troops as prisoners of war, and I thought it must be him. I never knew whether it was or not."

Her suitor was likely Jacob Voorhies, who was born in 1795 and served in the Tennessee senate. But because he would have been close to her age, by 1865 he would have been old to have fought in the Civil War. Whoever he was, someone by the name of Voorhies was wounded at Nashville with the Forty-eighth Tennessee Infantry in 1864—and of course he was a Rebel. He was probably a William Voorhies, whose military career ended in capture.

19

Rascals

Catharine's uncles urged her to marry Mr. Voorhies, but luckily she didn't. Years later, one of the uncles, Franceway Cossitt, writes to her of Voorhies's bad character, reassuring her she didn't make a mistake in refusing him. Her uncle Franceway was the beloved Aunt Charlotte's brother and thus one of the younger siblings of her mother, Anne, and by now lived in Elkton, Kentucky, a region still fervent with religious activity. He was a Presbyterian minister, and eventually one of the founders of Cumberland College. He was a good uncle to Catharine.

She kept one letter received from Uncle Franceway about Mr. Voorhies that is interesting for the light it sheds on the ubiquitous American figure, the con man. Voorhies had taken the whole family in: "From the time of his going to North Carolina till the death of our loved Charlotte, I was constantly lending them money, until they were in my debt about 800 dollars."

Franceway goes on indignantly about Voorhies's attempts to slander him, his involvement with other women, and his general seediness.

I can now see, he never showed the least disposition to pay me. I then thought he was honest, and rested contentedly with fair promises. After Sister's death, when he was receiving a salary of 800 dollars per year, I thought he might pay me, particularly as he was convinced that I knew he had the money, and he knew I had been building a brick

house in Town, was in want of money, and depended on him
to pay me. Many people advised me to sue him and told me
they believed he intended to defraud me. I would not believe them and thought them all his enemies.

Uncle Franceway was to be taken in further—the scalawag
talked him into trusting him again and again, and told him he,
Jacob Voorhies, would accept some of Franceway's debts instead
of giving Franceway the money; but then when people presented
their bills to Voorhies, he implied that it was Franceway who
had defrauded them.

How the stories flew like lightening that Parson Cossitt had
defrauded such and such a man, and even his brother-in-
law did not pretend to deny it. Everybody wondered—they
would not have thought it—they had thought him a good
man—what will become of the cause of religion if preachers
conduct so?
  I took a favorable opportunity to vindicate my own
character, and after much debate, he owned that I drew the
orders on him by agreement and he was actually owing me
the sum. But still would not pay me. My honour was fully
vindicated and everybody saw that he had behaved like a
bad man, and they knew that I must have seen it. Now, those
who were afraid of injuring my feelings before, were em-
boldened to tell me of his intemperance. My wife had often
heard it and told me of it, but I did not believe it.
  At length I met him at the house of a Mr. Smith. He there
gave me very abusive language, in so much that Mr. and Mrs.
Smith said they would never invite him to their house again.
He told several things which he knew, and I knew to be lies,
some of which Mr. Smith said he knew to be lies, from what

Mr. Voorhies had told him before. He now saw he had offended Mr. Smith's family, and had not succeeded in making them despise me as he had intended. He saw there was no hope of making up the matter with me, and he went about saying every thing he could to injure me. Never was a man more unsuccessful, for he only added to the multitude of his enemies.

Uncle Franceway, urged by his friends to sue, did recover some three hundred dollars, but then Voorhies slipped away to "the province of Texas." Franceway says he could almost be glad his sister had died and thus been spared all this humiliation, though maybe it wouldn't have happened if she had lived: "He loved her, and what is more, he feared her. She had all their concerns under her management. It was very plain that her superior mind directed all."

He recounts more of Mr. Voorhies's iniquities, for example, after his wife Charlotte's death, he strung along a respectable girl to the point that her parents were preparing the wedding.

"But I have said enough!" Uncle Franceway goes on to describe some of his own personal triumphs—preachings and conversions—fifty over the weekend! And hopes Catharine will be spared from falling under the influence of the Arian and Socinian heresies that he'd heard were making some headway in her area—these were mildly divergent views of the Trinity or of Jesus' divinity.

20

The Elusive Eleazer

One wonders if Catharine regretted her decision to remain true to her choice, because in 1826 Eleazer was still far from being an ardent suitor. She writes:

> After Dr. Martin left Vermont, it was more than a year, I think near a year and a half before I received a letter from him, and then not till I wrote him.
>
> After waiting nearly a year and hearing nothing from Dr. Martin, I wrote to my cousin Lavinia Stebbins of W[illiamstown] to find out where he was, if she could, [ask] of some of his relatives, without letting them know that I wanted the information. How long the time seemed to me, while I heard nothing from him. I tried to be cheerful, and had very pleasant company of young ladies, and I might say some beaus, but I kept them at a distance, all but one. . . .
>
> Some time after I wrote to my cousin, she wrote me Dr. Martin was in Ohio and his Post Office address was Duffs Fork, Fayette County, Ohio.

She takes the bull by the horns and writes forthrightly to the young doctor, and finally gets a letter back from Strafford, Vermont, where he has been sick, presumably with that bilious fever:

> Indeed my life was for a time despaired of, but Catharine I should not have died without friends for the family with whom I board were extremely kind & the lady of the house

watched over me as though I had been her own son . . .
through their goodness under the All wise Ruler of human
events I am again restored to perfect health, but at that
time I did not fear nor can I say I dreaded death; this no
doubt was a stoic stupidity.

Roaming alone the little towns of New England, he'd become
depressed. He had been looking for a place to practice, had tried
and abandoned several possibilities because of the climate or
the lack of patients:

> But Catharine, it was when I thought of Marriage that my
> present circumstances and future prospects staring me full
> in the face seemed to forbid the accomplishment of my de-
> sires.

He goes on to recount, somewhat tactlessly, how the young
ladies of the neighborhood vie for his attention.

Catharine says:

> So I wrote to him telling him if he wished to dissolve our
> engagement, he should say so and not keep me in ignorance
> of his whereabouts so long, for I gave him his liberty and if
> he wished it, to say so and I should not hold him to any of
> his engagements to me. And I further told him that Mr. V
> had made proposals and my dear uncle had written to me
> about it, but I told them I had long been engaged to Dr. M.
> and could not accept another, but had sent Mr. Voorhies my
> likeness, as he had never seen me, and I supposed Dr. M.
> did not care for it.

Eleazer protests his sincerity:

Catharine you are what I ever found you to be, an exception to the rest of your sex, true as the needle to the pole, and Catha‹ rine believe me while you remain single you shall never hear that my hand is given were you here. O! Catharine, it would consummate my happiness to give you a legal right to call me so; believe me Catharine had I not been more of a stoic I should not have suffered less than yourself, since our separation.

Would you and I believe a man who talked like this? He goes on protesting:

I acknowledge the neglect of which you complain & if what I have written can not plead my excuse I must throw myself on your mercy & plead for pardon, for I know there has been a strange inconsistency in my conduct; for want of room, I can hardly notice your letter but only thank you for the kindness it manifests; for Catharine it is only yourself that is capable of such exalted sentiments . . . but suffer me to subscribe myself your sincere friend and Lover.

Catharine had little choice but to accept his apologies. In her recollection:

In the beginning of the year 1826 I received a long letter from him, telling me of his long journey west, his sickness and low spirits—and how if he was out of the way I might be riding in my carriage and be happy in the south and not share his poverty. But when he could collect enough to come East, he would come and marry me, if I was still will‹ ing to have him.

He said the Country where he was, was very new and the people, mostly from old Virginia, Mariland and Kentucky, of the lower class and very rough and uncouth and different from what I had been accustomed to. He had not intended to stay there, and if I was willing to share it with him, when he was through with the fall practice he would start the early part of the winter and make his friends a visit in New England and come and marry me. So of course I expected him.

How much history is compressed in that summary? With how much sewing and waiting for letters and anxious despair did she pass the winter months? How much more mud did Eleazer have to slog through, mud a principal hazard for a country doctor?

He continued to write me throu' the summer, but did not start so early in the winter for home as he had intended, on account of the Mrs. G, who had nursed him so faithfully. She had a long sickness that winter and was near dying and probably would if she had not had a doctor near her. So he started some time in Feb. 1827 and rode throu' Ohio to a neighborhood near Buffalo, where he had acquaintance, and left his horse there and took the stage. When he got to Vermont, the snow was near three feet deep and in crossing the mountains the passengers would have to get out and walk and help lift the Stage out of the drifts of snow, throu' the latter part of March.

He visited his friends in Williamstown and did not come up to Hatley [one of the villages, with Stanstead and Granby, where various family members lived, an area associated with Loyalists from the United States] until the middle of April. I had just got to sit up after having the measles very hard, but as I had my dress and clothes all ready, we were married on the 20th of April 1827, but did not start from home for a week or more after.

Wedding Journey

It's 1827. The newly married Catharine and Eleazer set off on their wedding trip in April, intending to settle in Ohio. Eleazer had arrived in Stanstead to marry her, but had taken his time, it seemed to her, stopping to visit relatives, staying away until late spring when the snows had mostly melted and travel was easier. She had readied her clothes for the wedding journey; she'd been waiting, in a way, nine years; she was now twenty-six, not quite old enough to have been thought an old maid, but still an age where her relatives felt relieved at this outcome.

Catharine's description of their wedding journey throws some light on the difficulties of travel, though they had the use of the new Erie Canal:

> We made a visit in W. [?] for two weeks or so, and while there, Dr. Elias Smith, who was raised in the same neighborhood with my husband and had settled in the Eastern part of Ohio (but now lives in Racine, Wis.). He came home and was married to Judge Lind's daughter. We were at their wedding and we all came on together to the Reserve, as that part of Ohio was called. Then we had to hire a man to carry us down to Fayette Co. in his own wagon. We had come on the Canal through [New] York State but we were I think about three weeks getting to Yankeetown from Vermont.

These first settlers brought their stuff on wagons or in hired stagecoaches—books and bedclothes, musical instruments, clocks, with such culture and memorabilia as they could transport. They were poor, and they moved a lot; when one place or another didn't work out, there was another a few miles away. Reading Eudora Welty's *Delta Wedding*, I was struck by the similarities between this midwestern life and the life she described in the Deep South; Bloomingburg, Watseka, and Chenoa had (and still have) far more in common with Welty's Mississippi community than with Chicago and cities to the north, especially before the fatal rift of the rebellion.

The families who came to Watseka or Bloomfield or Bloomingburg back in the 1820s and still live around there were perhaps unaware they formed part of a migration worth a name, the Yankee migration, a stream of people moving in search of new opportunity, new land, the possibility of luck. These first settlers might have come from either America or Canada or both, for in that era the English-speaking people seemed not to pay much attention to the borders. During the War of 1812, with the Revolution so recently over (1783) and Indian wars continuing, British commanders complained that the settlers whose cooperation they needed for supplies would help neither the British nor the American forces; they were too busy just protecting their henhouses from marauding soldiers from both sides.

Settlers had been flocking to the Midwest after the Land Act of 1820, which established favorable conditions for buying land from the U.S. government for two dollars an acre, on credit. But the territories of Ohio, Indiana, and Illinois were still rough, largely agricultural, and not free of Indian unrest. The homesteaders were planning to till the land, but folks like Catharine and Eleazer were the support system—doctors, preachers, blacksmiths, and the like coming along after the farmers. When the newlyweds landed in western New York, then eastern Ohio, to Yankeetown, they were among a huge number of other people making this journey, following the westward movement, mostly for economic reasons, but there was a spirit too of adventure and possibility.

When Catharine and Eleazer were looking for a place to settle, Eleazer had checked out Kentucky, but reported that the people there were not the kind of people she was used to, they were "rough." Eleazer's reference to the people of Kentucky being of a "lower class" or "rough" is interesting: What social class did they belong to? Was it a class-conscious society?

When I grew up in Moline, it never occurred to me that I was a member of either a social class or an ethnic group—these were simply not the categorical terms in use. Thus I was amused but also rather shocked only a few years ago to come across a book by Florence King called *Wasp, Where Is Thy Sting?*, about the ethnic group now called WASPs—Catharine and Eleazer, but also me. I had the eerie feeling King had peeked at my shopping list, beheld my child-rearing practices and style of cookery. To forget the plastic bag of giblets inside the roasting chicken—I thought it happened to everyone; who knew it was an ethnic trait? It was strange to feel that you are not only a member of an ethnic group but a typical member, exhibiting characteristics people can caricature with some accuracy and often deplore, like the famous "coldness." One example is found in WASP mothering styles; in some groups, says King, the mother bursts into tears at the idea that her son is leaving home, but the WASP mother buys him a Eurail pass. It's absolutely true, and we got Eurail passes for our daughters too.

However, King distinguishes between High WASPs and Low ones. The former refers to rich people on the Eastern Seaboard,

and the latter to what get called hillbillies and rednecks. Catharine and Eleazer were neither of those, but somewhere in between, on the modest side, in a limbo of schoolteachers, farmers,
doctors, the occasional minister. These are still the usual paths
in our family, as if Americans were stuck in hereditary castes,
like Indian woodcutters or Thai marionettists.

The newlywed couple lights on Bloomingburg, in Ohio:

> And a desolate looking country it was to me. It was near
> Deer Creek, where most of the timber grew, and the people
> had cleaned the timber for half a mile around, so they might
> cultivate the ground, with 4 houses. But when I would ride
> on horse back up in the level prairie, and it looked so lonely
> and forsaken all round the 3 or 4 houses (barrens, they called
> it) there was plenty of roses and other wild flowers, I thought
> it a beautiful country and especially because there were no
> hills to climb and no stones, but a rich clay soil.

This was where they found a tworoom shack that brought
her to tears. This was the future—this was what she had left
home, and cast her lot with a stranger for.

> The Doctor had, before going east, spoke for a house in a
> small village called Bloomingburg, people mostly from York
> State and Pennsylvania, about 8 miles from Deer Creek.
> But . . . another young Dr. had bought it and gone to prac
> tice there, so he saw no other way but to stay where we were.
> So he rented a small house with two rooms and a back shed.
> He bought some secondhand furniture, as there was none
> made or kept there, or in B[loomingburg].

He had put up 2 or 3 little shelves near the chimney for me to put my crockery upon. When we got what few things we could get put to rights, I sat down and had a cry.

He came in and found me crying, stood and looked at me a few moments and then said, "Well, Catharine, there is one thing to comfort you. No one who ever knew you in former days will ever come here to see you or know how you are fixed, and as soon as we can we will get something better."

I did feel glad that none of my former acquaintance could know how I was fixed in that new country.

22

Bloomingburg

Catharine describes the population they found in 1826 when she and her new husband got to Ohio:

> Well settled up from New England, though long before I left [Canada], many English and Scotch had come there, bought the farms, many of them, and they had moved back to the United States. Since I came to Illinois, I find several families who came from Canada were born and raised in Stanstead, my native place. Judge Marriman, the Packers, and I believe some of the Ives, though not all of them.

Bloomingburg, like my mother's town of Watseka and its fellow little town, Chenoa, are villages in flat farm country—typical midwestern villages. Towns like those where my mother and father grew up, or where I grew up, far from any ocean, had first been settled by these East Coast people moving west, like Catharine and Eleazer, little places in Ohio, Illinois, Indiana, Kentucky, Tennessee, and Iowa, wherever there was farmland to be cleared, or a doctor or clergyman or schoolteacher needed.

Eventually families became more stationary, implanting themselves in a town and in the surrounding towns and farms, like crop circles or rust, spreading out, marrying out, but not moving so far or so often. Eventually they couldn't help marrying in—everyone was a cousin or connection and so it remains to this day. Where you own property, you tend to stay, *settle* is the usual word, with its hint of sedimentary dullness. Thus was the Midwest settled in little towns like Bloomingburg, or Chenoa and Watseka. People had always come from somewhere else, sometimes trying other towns along the way. Restless and hopeful, driven out—Catharine doesn't discuss why they would leave one place to live first here, then there. It was a westward impulse, it was economics. The whole population seemed on the move. But her girlhood had been a series of dislocations, living with this relative, then that, boarding or taking in boarders; it was a nation of people moving around, and she was used to it.

If the surly note in the political climate of today comes from a wish that things could be the way they used to be, we should look backward closely, to see how they actually were—turbulent, mostly unsettled, and primitive, but also cooperative and optimistic.

23

Women's Work: Quilts

Of course there were women in all these early stories. Ranna married Ruth Porter, though we know nothing about her except that she made him promise not to go back to France. There was Anne Cole with her brine recipe. On the whole subject of women's work, I would come to have a nuanced view after I found the diaries of my great-grandmothers and saw that though women then had lives full of responsibility and respect, their positions were earned by ceaseless toil and poignant cares, especially the deaths of children, of all sorrows surely the worst. But despite my dislike of *Little Women,* this book could be partly about the happiness of women like the March girls, happy despite their troubles—happy sewing, making quilts and jam, back in the day when such things were necessary and valued.

Catharine mentions several times that as a girl, she went to this or that household to sew bonnets, evidently for a wage or for her keep. When she went to stay with an aunt and help with sewing, certainly room and board were involved, and perhaps a small wage too. It's undoubted that Catharine and probably aunts and friends sewed her wedding wardrobe. And when their dresses and cloaks wore out, the usable bits would become quilt patches. She describes housekeeping in the 1830s: "Though I always had hired help (except now and then a week or two) yet I had a plenty to do with so many to come and go, my fruit to dry, preserve and make apple butter and quince and plum, meats to take care of, candles to make etc. etc. We could not run to the grocery as we do here and get whatever we wanted."

She doesn't dwell on the fact that sometimes ten people were living in her household; the laundry for such a number was done by hand in boiling water, sheets ironed, endless dinners cooked, all the clothes homemade—a life barely different from her mother's childhood life at the end of the eighteenth century.

Quilted by Aunt Henrietta

I've brought with me to Paris one quilt made by my aunt Henrietta, whom we called Aunt Bappy; there are others at home in San Francisco, made by her or by Aunt Martha, Aunt Ruth, or my mother. When I was a little girl, Mother gave me quilt pieces to patch—I could barely sew, so they were crooked and inept, and by the time I was a teenager I'd given up; but the few squares that were finished I wish I had now, to remember the simple pattern of

blocks, and what colors we used. Quilts are an art form of considerable elegance, and if nothing else encourage patience.

As a young wife, I finished a simple quilt made from worn-
out dresses I liked and sentimental bits from the children's
clothes. Alas, like memories themselves, that quilt disappeared
from a beach house we had, where I'd left it. I should have put it
away, as women carefully did put away such family treasures.

Some quilt tops I've inherited from my aunts remain to be
joined to their backs, stuffed, and quilted. I did one myself, blue
and white "Goose and Goslings," but did it so badly that I plan
to consign the rest to one of the groups of women who quilt to
benefit their churches or schools—when I find such a group.
Aunt Bappy's quilt in Paris is a Hawaiian quilt, that is, the design is appliquéd onto the blocks—in this case, oak leaves, yellow on white, with the same oak-leaf pattern used for the quilting
stitches. Then, as now, the ladies had books of quilting designs,
but were glad and proud to find or invent a new one.

There are some who say that quilts played a role in the management of the Underground Railroad to help runaway slaves
escape; certain patterns, hung in windows or over railings, would
signal safety for flight, or post a warning. I looked into this, and
would like to think it's true, but the evidence is not very convincing. Still, the tradition exists and must have been based on
something.

When my aunt Martha died, we had to get rid of things in
her very big house in Chenoa. One of its rooms was a sewing
room—there was a sewing room in Watseka too; these were
troves of trimmings, patterns, buttons, rows of lace and snaps
and fringes, enough to last me for any sewing project I might
think of in the future, and also my daughters. They like to sew,

and I imagine this is a tradition that has come straight down to us from Anne and Catharine, along with, perhaps, some of these very fringes, things you can't find anymore, some rusty black by now, some tarnished gold, the sequined pockets and epaulets as glittery as ever on fragile, deteriorating webs of mesh.

I've saved some of the shredded silk dresses from the sewing room too, with the idea of taking them apart to copy the patterns, though I've yet to do it. One of them, my grandmother's wedding dress, fit me when I was a small twelve·year·old, a tiny garment. Some of the dresses were made by my grandfather's sister, Great· aunt Lottie (named for Anne's sister Charlotte, mentioned above), who lived in the house before Aunt Martha did, and was the one who stored portraits in her attic of Catharine Anne and Eleazer Martin, oil paintings dated 1849 that I have now.

Painting and quilting and canning were activities still found in the lives of my mother and her sisters in the twentieth cen· tury, and are the reason midwestern girls can knit and sew and quilt, unlike some of our big·city friends. The generals' wives, Mrs. Baum and Mrs. Rolfe, were perfect in the womanly arts, because, just as in the centuries past, their survival had de· pended on them—their husbands had to keep a good table and provide splendid hospitality in order to rise.

My aunts, all of them, always seemed to me to be busy mak· ing things—canning and quilting, knitting and crocheting— activities carried over from the preindustrial agricultural world in which they still seemed to live, though only Aunt Grace, Aunt Pearl, and Aunt Goldie still actually lived on farms. For a while Aunt Grace had an outhouse instead of indoor plumbing, a circumstance of greatest shame to me, and dread too when on one of our visits I would have to use it.

From the example of my mother and aunts, serene with their quilting and watercolors, and their apparatus for canning vegetables and jam, it seemed to me as a child that women had the more enjoyable lot in life. Now I see that there is something to be said for and against either condition, but—somewhat seditiously, for of course like any nice woman I am a feminist—I still prefer women's tasks, and think them both easier and more interesting.

But I was aware, growing up, that people like us were in some kind of transitional period between an old-fashioned world and another modern, different one where people didn't make things by hand. Some of my friends did not have parents who made things, but instead kept themselves busy going to doctors, and tried to invest lives that bored them with interest in Kiwanis or golf—I thought of them as modern parents. The time would come when the moms could have paying jobs, but it didn't come to my mother and her friends, and I'm not sure they would have liked paying jobs. My mother seemed to have plenty to do, volunteering in the 1940s and through the war and throughout her life, with her endless projects of jam and sewing, bookbinding and making clothes—serious projects that were taken seriously. All this was just at the beginning of television, of course.

They all seemed to me to be happy women leading useful lives, and were spared the discontent that Betty Friedan would later discuss people having, a population she defined as overqualified and underappreciated, college-educated, postindustrial city women still caught by the idea that women needed to stay home homemaking if their husbands could afford it, when they would have preferred to have jobs. I believe my aunts considered that they did have jobs, and quilts and housedresses and hot pads were part of it. Housedresses first, that is, that would become, eventually, hot pads and quilts. The tart apples from the backyard became applesauce, and the pie cherries became pies if the birds didn't get them.

In some ways, life could be harder for men, as it was for Eleazer Martin.

Portrait of Dr. Eleazer Martin

24

Eleazer the Doctor

After finishing medical school, in Hanover, New Hampshire—
apparently Dartmouth—studying with older doctors, Catharine's new husband, Eleazer, then had to seek a place to practice.
At one point he had written to Catharine of what a struggle
it was:

> After I left you I returned to Williamstown where I cer-
> tainly did not do business well enough to pay my board. I
> hoped to find a better situation in NY and big with expec-
> tation and elated with hope left my native state, left my Fa-
> ther's house, Father, Mother, Sisters, Brothers all dear as the
> ties of blood and their unlimited kindness toward me could
> make them. I say I left all these in better spirits and more
> buoyant feelings than I had felt for months before in their
> society with the prospects I then had before me. . . .

By the time of his death in 1874 he had spent more than forty
years as a country doctor in this region of Ohio and then Illinois.
Even after they were established, the life of a small-town midwestern doctor in the mid-nineteenth century was difficult and
frustrating, for him and for his family. He would be gone days at
a time on his circuit, riding a horse, or sometimes taking a wagon.
When there was an epidemic, or a family stricken with illness, he
would be expected to tend them, and often slept at the houses of
the people he was treating, or in a nearby inn. Treatment was
limited to bleeding, sponging with water, and "cupping"—a

strange process of applying suction cups to the exterior of the body over the possibly ailing interior organs; there were various tinctures and herbs, including cocaine. Sometimes people got better.

Catharine tells many stories about Eleazer's cases, some pretty harrowing, as when their daughter Charlotte [named after the beloved Aunt Charlotte, who had married the scoundrel Voorhies] arrived with a one/year/old boy belonging to her sister Mary, who was confined with a new baby.

> The dear little fellow, I seem to see him yet. He was not well, and the Dr. found he had abscesses of the bowels one after another, which was very painful while gathering and the dear little thing would cry night and day, but when one began to discharge he would then seem more quiet until another one began to gather, so he was in my arms most of the day and night. I slept but little all that six months he was with us. Five or six weeks of the last of the time Mary was with us, but she had a babe to take care of. . . . Dr. Martin and his [the baby's] uncle Dr. [William] Elder did all they could do, but he died in January, about one and a half years old.

The toll of constant childbearing and infant and maternal deaths seems unimaginably high and unendurable. Catharine herself bore nine children, and outlived all of them but the Mary mentioned above—Mary Elder, the wife of Charles Stewart Elder, who was off in the Civil War.

Eleazer was a doctor, and so was this son/in/law, Charles Stewart, and so were their brothers, the other doctor Elder Catharine mentions above, and one of Eleazer's brothers, still back east. Doctors still run in the family—I've been married to two of them, my

brother is one, one of our ex-sons-in-law, and so on. My long association with this profession has caused me to respect doctors,
mostly, especially their human capacity for empathy and wish to
heal. But it must have been an especially taxing profession in the
mid-nineteenth century, when there was so little you could do for
people, and death was omnipresent, forever reminding you of piti-
less, fragile biology and your personal powerlessness.

Many of the anecdotes Catharine tells give a glimpse of the
daily role sickness and death played in everybody's lives. Eleazer
had a nephew named Burroughs, a widower with a young son, living in Bloomington, Illinois, a town nearby. When Burroughs married a young widow who had been sewing for Catharine and
Eleazer, he and his new wife moved to "Martin town, Illinois," a
little town not far away, leaving the son in Bloomington, "sick for
two months or more, without any friends with him, except what
the young men did for him who roomed in the same block
and boarded at the Hotel." Charles Stewart Elder, Catharine's
son-in-law, who was studying medicine at the time, and his brother,
Dr. William Elder, sent for Eleazer to help. Catharine also helped:

> When I heard how he was situated I went up with my hus-
> band, prepared to stay several days, but only stayed two
> days and returned with my husband as he was not willing I
> should be from home. He said he would write to [young
> Burroughs's] father, as he did not know that he was so sick,
> but I did all I could for him, bathed him and changed his
> clothes etc. His father came down directly and stayed two
> weeks with him, but could not leave his business any longer,
> so he borrowed a cot bed and lifted him onto that and some
> gentlemen helped . . . carry him on that to the cars and he

fetched him to our house on it, and the next day went home
and left him for us to care for.

About that time, Governor Martin's only child Annette
came to visit us from Vermont and stayed a year. She and
Charlotte were quite a help about taking care of him, keeping off flies etc. He had been there, I think, about four weeks
and one day I thought he was dying and sent for Dr. Mahan,
as Dr. M was gone. He gave him some stimulants which re-
vived him a little, and when Dr. got home, he said he could
not live long. So McCurdy got on the night train and went to
Iroquois [County to tell the father] and his father came down
the next morning.

But he lived, I think, about three days, and passed away.

How often, it seemed, there was a dying relative upstairs, or a
relative come to stay a year or two, boarders, people coming to
sew. Catharine mentions several illnesses she or Eleazer suffered
themselves or were involved in helping the sufferer, sometimes for
months. When Catharine expected Eleazer to come to marry her
in early 1827, instead he was delayed by the illness of a close
friend. You tended sick friends, they tended you; you convalesced
for weeks or months. Some of the things were very hard to diag-
nose in retrospect:

That year I had a very severe spell of billious fever and got
dreadfully salived and like to have died. My teeth were all
loose, and I lay three weeks with a bowl under my mouth to
catch the Saliva. But when I got well, I was better of my liver
complaint and dispepsia than I had been for several years.

What can that have been?

25

Sorrow

Within a year of her marriage, with the fated fertility of women then, Catharine had her first baby, and named her Catharine Anne, after herself. They called her Sissie. This baby was followed by Charlotte Augusta in 1830 and Martha Olivia in 1831. When they were one, three, and five years old, all three little girls died in the space of a week or two:

The Scarlet Fever had been very fatal among the children off in various neighborhoods in the country around the village at certain periods, for 2 or 3 years, and I was very much afraid of it, as the Dr. was among it a great deal. Though we had heard of none for several months, it came into our place in March 1833 and was very fatal. Our dear little prattlers were the first to take it.

I wrote March above, but it was February, a little before my oldest child was 5 years old. The school house was right near on the public square, and we let our oldest one go to school. One day an older girl came leading my little Anne in and said she was sick and had been vomiting. I laid her on the bed and could see she was very sick. My husband had gone over to Deer Creek and had not returned though it was the second day after he left home.

There happened to be an old Dr. from Washington, the county seat in town that day—as the Dr. was gone, some one had sent for him, and I called him in. He did what he thought best and toward night, Dr. Martin came home. But I think she went into spasms before he came and continued in them till she died, which was 30 hours from when she was fetched home.

After she was buried, the second one, Augusta (we called her Gussie), cried several times to have us go and fetch home her dear Sissie Anne and not leave her in the ground. We had carried her to the burying of her sister. I tried to make her understand that it was only the body that was in the ground, that her Soul or spirit had gone to God and was alive and would live in heaven with God, but what could a child only two and a half years old understand about death and Heaven? But it seemed to comfort her. A week or two after her [Anne's] death, I gave her a piece of sugar to eat. She eat part of it and laid away the rest very carefully in her drawer. I said to her, Gussie, why don't you eat your sugar? Don't lay it away. She looked up at me very pleasant and says, "Ma I will save it until I die and go to heaven and carry it to my dear Sissie Anne." And several times when she had sugar eating, she would lay it away and answer me in the same words, or nearly so.

About six weeks after Anne's death, little Martha Olivia commenced vomiting, after an hour or two went into spasms and died in 23 hours from when she was taken sick. She died early in the morning and was buried that evening, as they did not keep them long after death then in Ohio. Before she was buried I got so bad with the Scarlet Fever that I could not go to the burying of my dear one. I was very bad. They could see the very bad inflammation down my sore throat, but it never came outside till the 9th or tenth day. I remember the Dr. sat by me two days thinking I should die.

I think it was Friday and Saturday after the little one was buried, Mr. Gregory was sick and sent for him. I think on Friday, but he could not leave me. On Saturday, little Augusta, who had been very sober after her youngest sister died—I had never seen her laugh, came to her pa and says pa, do play with me. He took her by the hands and hopt and jumpt her round a few minutes, and she laughed and giggled, and thought it was quite a treat to have pa play with her.

I looked at them, and the thought came into my mind, "poor little dear, that is the last play you will have."

And sure enough, it was. Sunday morning I felt better, and told the Dr. he had better go and see his old friend Mr. G., as he would be waiting for him. So after breakfast, he went. It was a pleasant spring morning, the first of April. I had a cousin with me who had come from the East the year before, Clarisse Cossitt. She was walking in the yard with my little girl; they came in, and Cousin [Clarisse] says "Cousin Augusta says I must take off her shoes and lay them up on the beam on the back porch with her dear little Sissie Anne and little Martha Olivia's, and lay her in the cradle. She is going to have the Scarlet Fever now, and die and go to God, and live in Heaven with her dear, sweet little sisters." (She never spoke of them after their death without calling them dear or sweet.)

I said, "don't say so, I can't spare you."

"Yes, I am ma," she said. "Take me up Coussie and take off my shoes," and she repeated over the same words she had said in the yard and then added "lay me in the cradle, Cous-sie." She [Clarisse] took off her shoes and laid her in the cra-dle and rocked her a few minutes. She slept a half hour and waked up vomiting, and I knew she was going then, as she had said. Mr. George Fullerton mounted his horse and went directly after Dr. Martin. She lived 6 or 7 days. He sponged her in cool water, and it came outside, but O! how dark and angry it looked. She lay in spasms two days and nights. O! I thought I could not see her die in such agony as the others had, and I prayed to God to relieve her suffering and let her die more gently than the others had. And she did come out of her fits and lived two days after it and died peacefully and I felt to say "Thy will O God be done, not mine." I was getting better, and could sit up some, when the last one died, but was not able to go to the burying.

When I got up, my house was empty, three little prattlers all gone, not one left.

26

Depression

Dr. Eleazer could not save his little girls Sissie Anne, Martha, or Gussie, nor four of those who came after. He led his life of driving his buggy (supposedly with fugitive slaves hidden inside) or riding his horse through mud—mud recurs in midwestern recollections with much frequency; he tried to save people, but was mostly used to seeing them die, for there wasn't really much you could do most of the time. It was a hard life, and it is no wonder he was often depressed, had suffered from "low spells" ever since his and Catharine's courting days, and had never been free of them. What with the deaths, the sickness, slavery, Eleazer was given to these spells, when he wouldn't speak, or said horrible things to Catharine. After twenty-five years of life together, she confronted him: "I knew it was the loss of our children that made him so unlike himself, but he seemed to forget that I had to bear the same affliction and greaf & also his aberration of mind, & poverty, as that seemed to press upon his mind—that we three were going to bring him to poverty, though he owned that large farm" and a lot of other things she lists.

> I never disputed him when he found fault or got in a quarrel with him, but <u>prayed God</u> to give me the grace to bear it, said as little to him & told no one of my trouble . . . but his spells would come on and made me very unhappy, but I kept it from . . . everybody who might have suspected his difficulties.
>
> When he was finding fault with us [their daughter Mary and Catharine's mother, Anne, who by then was living with them, Mr. Meyrick having died] his eyes would glare and seem

to spark and look fairly green, like he ought to be in a lunitik Assilum. If he was a little sick, he would lie down, grone all over, wish he could die and wish he was dead, he did not want to live any longer, & many times I was very much afraid he would kill himself.

A nephew spending one summer with them told Catharine that Eleazer was "as much like his father as could be, and he did kill himself."

When his fits were over, she would try to reason with him that they had plenty of money, God could help him, and so on. Finally:

One day when we were alone & he had one of his low-spirited spells & rather finding fault with me & all the rest, I heard him awhile. I then sat down and said:

"My dear husband, you have talked awhile, now stop and hear me." He stopped and looked astonished, so I told him how he had been ever since the loss of our children & had made me and the girls very, very unhappy, forgetting that I, too, had to bear the sorrow of their death & all of his low spirits and fault-finding. Had come to Lexington [a new town near Bloomington], very much against my own feelings & judgment, in hopes it would make him more happy.

I have born this unhappy life for some 8 years most of the time. Now I am determined it is not my duty to live so any longer. If you cannot restrain your own feelings & keep from making me so unhappy, just give me a few thousand dollars, just enough for me & Charlotte to live upon & you may live where you please and see if you can be any happyer. I don't want any divorce or any noise about it but if you can't restrain your feeling, let Charlotte & I live alone. I know you have property enough to make us all comfortable.

Even to mention divorce in that era must have taken not
only courage but imagination, for it was not often done. (Mine
in 1965 was the first divorce on either side of the family.) Eleazer
said nothing, but after this either he changed his ways or she did
not have the will to leave, for she says nothing more to suggest
their married life had not been happy.

Maybe none of them was ever happy. Maybe life in general
was not happy then, though I think, maybe, that I am happy, in
general, and lucky as well, and I hope this is what most people
end up thinking, that the life they have is the best option and
that they've had a bit of luck. He didn't kill himself after all, and
at the end, which came for him in 1874, turned to religion, at
least enough to satisfy Catharine.

27

Wars

It seems Americans are always at war. From the beginning of American history, wars have curled and smoked around us. The first arrivals from Europe, like Ranna Cosset, tried not to get mixed up in the North American conflicts raging among the British, French, Indians, and American settlers, but even so, Ranna was captured like a pawn between the French and British during the Queen Anne's War. Ranna's sons didn't have a war; among his grandsons, some fought in the Revolution, but some went to Canada, prefiguring what people would do during the war in Vietnam. The Revolutionary War was a reality to Anne and Ambrose Cossitt, the parents of Anne Perkins. Anne's daughter Catharine would experience two wars.

Catharine thought of herself as having been mostly raised in Canada, but in fact during her girlhood, the exact political configuration of Lower Canada and the American border had yet to be decided. Besides the English and American, other forces were vying for political ascendancy—there was a large Irish population that dreamed of establishing a United Ireland in this American/Canadian inland region; and many people wanted to be neither Canadian nor American but citizens of a "Republic of Columbia," combining the two territories. Catharine writes about it:

In the winter of 15 or 16, I remember well when the peace was consummated between Great Britain and the United States, after the war of 1812. The stages in Claremont all came by with Peace, Peace written in large white letters on the outside. We in Stanstead had suffered very little inconvenience from the war, as Stanstead [Canada] and Derby [Vermont] people were neighbors, only divided by an imaginary line. I think they agreed not to disturb each other, though I remember there were troops on both sides sent there, but did not stay long, and people went either way across the line without any trouble.

These early midwesterners had left Europe behind them, though one of the earlier Rannas, the Tory uncle who settled in Canada, had gone to England for his ordination as an Episcopal priest in the 1750s. Catharine wrote her memoir in 1876, a century after American independence, but in her childhood, many people were still alive who had fought in both the War of 1812 and the Revolutionary War (she would also live through the Civil War). America was a hundred years old in 1876, and settlements by then had stretched far to the west of Illinois, into Iowa and Kansas, all the way to California, an empire for which Europe was insignificant and far away.

Apart from stories about their ancestor Ranna, there is no mention of Europe in the chronicles left by either Anne Perkins or Catharine Martin, and they are weak on the geography and history—they thought Ranna might have been the son of the Duke of Corsica, and that Robespierre might have been menacing him. The Napoleonic Wars, Restorations, the invasion of Paris by Prussians—all these had happened by Catharine's day, but they had few means of hearing what went on in the Old World, and seem to have cared less. In my childhood, people in

Watseka or Chenoa had long since left off wondering about what went on in the world outside; maybe this is still a midwestern mind-set, and, paradoxically, the greater urbanity offered by television now may have increased the impression that the outside world is a deplorable mass of tear gas and bombs.

Bloomingburg, Ohio, was a center of antislavery activity and a station of the Underground Railroad; and one of the chief organizers, William Dickey, was the pastor of the Presbyterian church the Martins attended at the time. Catharine writes about how the citizens of Ohio were very much divided in their feelings about slavery:

When the controversy about slavery was going around, there were round through the country many southerners and Kentuckeans who were very much opposed to Abolitionism. They even got up a public meeting in the country near Midway, and many agreed they would not carry butter or produce to Bloomingburg or employ an Abolitionist.

There was a neighborhood over the creek, where the farms were very low and wet and sickly, where Dr. Martin had practiced a great deal. Also an old man Green's family who lived near Midway . . . a Kentuckean [who] had a daughter married into a large family who lived over the Creek, and she lived near them. She and one or two or three of her husband's family were taken with fevers one fall, and Green persuaded them to have some other doctor, because he, Dr. Martin, was an Abolitionist.

The Dr. never noticed it, as he was very busy in another direction, where it was sickly [too]. After Green's daughter and three or four of the old folks family were dead, the youngest little girl took it and the old lady would have Dr. Martin, and she herself was taken with the same disease, and both very bad. But under Dr. Martin's treatment and a kind Providence, they both recovered. Green told an Abolitionist neighbor of this, that he did not like the Abs. because they helped the slaves away "on the underground railroad," as it was called. He was very bitter against them, but acknowledged that he had done wrong to Dr. Martin and said he never would lay a straw in his way again.

A few years after, he went down to visit his old home in Kentucky, and came home a good Abolitionist.

Unlike many family stories, which can come to seem more and more apocryphal the closer you look at them, the tradition in ours was also that some doctor forebear was a member of the Underground Railroad and carried escaping slaves in his buggy as he rode around tending his patients. This would be Eleazer.

It was above all the Civil War that marked the Midwest. The shade of Abraham Lincoln in his tall hat and the ghosts of Union soldiers and Confederate soldiers still stalk the cornfields of this region and steal along the rivers. My ideas about the Midwest had among their inspirations a sepia photograph of two young women in their late teens around 1880. They are in drag, wearing men's Civil War uniforms. The older girl, Great-aunt Lottie, wears an officer's uniform with many buttons and large epaulets; her sister Fanny is in what appear to be fatigues—gaiters and tight leggings, and a laced shirt. They're standing next to a Victorian chair that has come down to me.

Their parents, Mary and Charles Stewart Elder, were born in the 1830s, and Charles served in the Civil War, a war far from forgotten even now among people around Watseka, the way it

Lottie and her sister Fanny in Civil War drag

isn't forgotten in the South and must be remembered by anyone who tries to understand the Midwest or, indeed, America. In Moline, Chenoa, Watseka, there is a pervasive, quiet satisfaction with history, that Illinois has behaved so well in it, freeing the unfortunate slaves, and in my childhood during the Second World War that we would soon free the poor Europeans and terrified islanders trapped on map dots in the Pacific.

Across the Mississippi River from Moline are Davenport and Bettendorf, Iowa. The Mississippi at that point is three-quarters of a mile wide, and actually runs east and west, permanently damaging the sense of direction of many who grew up in the area. The Rock Island Arsenal, with the graves of Confederate soldiers who had been imprisoned there during the Civil War, was thrilling to us as little girls when we read in *Gone with the Wind* that Ashley Wilkes had been imprisoned there; and during the Second World War, it held Germans whom we thought we

Portrait of Charles Stewart Elder

saw occasionally on our way to the swimming pool, trimming bushes, wearing POW shirts. We were as conscious of the Civil War as of the world wars or perhaps even more so, with the Con· federate cemetery, and because we were, after all, in the Land of Lincoln, still under the spell of the tutelary presence, the fa· mous son of Illinois.

The curious photo of young women in Civil War drag prompted me to wonder, among other things, whose uniforms they were wearing. It was hardly usual for young women in small·town Illinois to dress in men's clothes. The two girls in uniform also reminded of how recent the Civil War was for peo· ple in the 1880s, only a little more remote than the first Iraq war is to us by now. The Civil War was very present even in my childhood (and dare I say still is, underlying the rancorous tones of Southern senators saying "Mah esteemed friend," and the scorn in the voices of the Northern ones as they talk to one an· other). On one side of my family, Eleazer Martin and Charles Stewart Elder were involved in it—these were great·great· grandfathers; but on the other side, I am the granddaughter of a Civil War veteran, a chronological aberration in my generation. This was my Lain grandfather, dead before I was born, who chased the rebels through Hacklebarney and Missouri with the Fourth Iowa Cavalry and married the colonel's daughter.

Great·great·grandmother Catharine in her chronicle doesn't say much about her son·in·law, great·grandfather Charles Stew· art Elder, off in the Civil War, but the Chenoa and Watseka rel· atives conserved artifacts, and even photographs, and memories retold of Lincoln's early days, and of Charles Stewart's service as a bandmaster with the Thirty·third Illinois Infantry out of Che· noa, Illinois. Just a few years ago I found his Civil War hat—a blue Stetson in perfect condition—in Aunt Martha's attic in Chenoa.

Midwestern states were far from unanimous about slavery. When I went to college in Missouri, right on the Mason-Dixon Line, the girls who came up from Savannah, or Mobile, or Jackson, Mississippi, brought with them their hoop skirts, Confederate hats and flags. These artifacts shocked me enormously. Before then, it hadn't occurred to me that there were still people who professed the values of the antebellum South; I had never heard that, or even seen instances of segregation, though before long, the civil rights movement would make us all aware of what still went on down there.

Wars have played a distinctly broadening role for midwesterners. My father was too old (and my brother too young) to have fought in the Second World War, but millions did, and my brother and my two husbands all did military service as doctors at the time of Korea and Vietnam.

As far as I know, my father and my uncles Ed and Bill on their troop ships in 1918 were the first of any of these prairie folk to find themselves aboard a ship on the sea. Going to sea had its perils even in the 1900s—my father hated the First World War troop ship and was sick the whole way—he complains that while on the trip over, he'd "lost about twenty-five pounds on the nine days trip."

However, what he mostly wrote home about was not the gruesome bloodshed—maybe soldiers generally leave such accounts to novelists and filmmakers. He wrote more often about where he went, far away, to distant lands—to Venice, for example. He often told about it, and wrote in his little memoir, "As a boy, I had always tried to imagine what a city with only water for streets would be like, and I quite well remember my first appearance there. It was a moonlit night when I stepped from the railroad station out on to the edge of the Grand Canal—really the culmination of my boyhood dreams." If you read only my father's account of how he and his friends blew all their pay on a sumptuous meal at the great Milanese restaurant Savini, and stayed in the Hotel Danieli in Venice, you would not think war was hell at all.

There's a sinister explanation for our ambivalent American militarism—it gets us out to see the world. Another compensation for my father, almost as thrilling to an Iowa boy as Europe, was landing in New York. In New York they had had to undergo delousing, though his regiment "had escaped the cooties the Western Front was noted for." Once deloused, they could go into New York City, where, just as in Rome he'd climbed the Spanish Steps ("just not on my knees") and visited the catacombs, now he saw other things most Iowa farm boys had not seen—Broadway shows, nightclubs, and restaurants.

I'm not sure he would have exchanged his war, any more than Charles Stewart Elder would have, finding his headaches disappeared, his appetite hearty. Charles writes from his Civil War encampment:

My dear Wife,
   Knowing that I shall not receive a letter from you until you hear from me I hasten to tell you of my whereabouts. We moved from Pilot Knob on Monday to this place (Ironton) which is about two miles south of the Knob and a much pleasanter place. We have a fine place for a camp with

shade and water and from the way things look at this time we shall stay here for some time. . . .

Camp life agrees with me splendidly. I can not eat enough to last me from one meal to another. My headache has not troubled me since I left home. We spread our blanket on the ground and wrap it around and sleep as sweet as babes.

He also writes home about the dances at his Union camp in Missouri:

I have not told you how I passed New Year's Eve, and I do not know as I had better tell, but I guess I will make a clean breast of it and tell you all about it. Some of the officers got up a dance at the headquarters hotel dining room. I was invited and made up my mind to go and enjoy myself as best I could. We had a splendid time. I danced with the Missouri girls to my heart's content. I did not tell them I was married, and I think I made an impression.

The local girls, he assures his wife, Mary, were not half as handsome as she. "However we danced until about two and broke off all sober and in good order." He wishes she were there, as some of the other wives were, but reckons it is just as well she was not, in case of attack, though he doesn't really sound too worried about that.

The Civil War band Charles organized in McLean County, the Thirty-third Illinois Volunteer Regiment Band, is still a musical group that plays at Illinois-related events at Arlington National Cemetery, or at Vicksburg reenactments. A bandmaster doesn't seem to me now very glamorous, though I learned that the bands were important in Civil War battles, drumming their

Charles Stewart Elder's Civil War band

troops into fighting spirit and acting as rallying points and direction finders for soldiers to follow, musicians as much in danger
of Confederate bullets as infantrymen were.

I haven't discovered what instrument he played, but another
detail emerged from the Web site of the present Thirty-third
Illinois musicians who claim him as a founder: a young lawyer,
Abraham Lincoln, came to Charles's wedding to Mary Martin in
1856. Catharine, his mother-in-law, doesn't mention this in her
memoir, though she does go into detail about Charles's struggles
to find a role in life before he studied medicine. It's clear she was a
little afraid her daughter Mary might have married a ne'er-do-well,
always borrowing money from Dr. Eleazer, her husband, and getting into debt, kind of like that scalawag Voorhies. It's lucky he
settled down to solid citizenry after the war.

IV

MODERN DAYS

28

Watseka, Chenoa

My father, Dolph Lain, had grown up on a farm near Bloomfield, Iowa, which was a long drive for us, or so it seemed to children squabbling in the backseat; but Mother was from nearer by, Watseka, Illinois, a three-hour drive from Moline eastward along the fields of brilliant green corn, or gaunt snow-covered bundles of stalks at Christmastime, to visit our numerous aunts and uncles. Thinking back on the life of Watseka and Chenoa in the days of my childhood, with only the *Chicago Tribune* and the radio to link them to the world (and the train to Chicago, for there were trains in those days), it was still a society that resembled, more than any other fictional equivalent I can think of, the one depicted by Jane Austen or Mrs. Gaskell, even in the 1950s still almost preindustrial, preoccupied with canning and quilting, a general store, print dresses, aprons, even wagons. Watseka and Chenoa might have been English villages, populated by the Weatherwaxes, Duckworths, Martins, Churchills, Lees, Binghams, Burnhams, Croswells, and Bells (to name some of my cousins), where the main activities were visiting and gossip. "Let's drive over to Pontiac to see Cousin Loralee," my aunt Henrietta would say. "We'll stop at Martha's on the way." Now they drove Packard cars instead of buggies, but the life was the same. They were late getting modern stoves; they were late getting televisions; they were late getting indoor plumbing on the farms.

Since coming to live there in the early nineteenth century, people in Chenoa and Watseka—in all these little Illinois

The Elder family. Front row: Henrietta, Frances, Martha;
back row: Tom, Grace, Edgar

towns—conducted lives they tried to live elegantly, according to memories of bygone grandeurs, and rules that drifted in from the great cities. In the bottom of a tiny purse I find one of Great-aunt Lottie's visiting cards: "Mrs. Lottie Elder Silliman," nicely engraved. Great-aunt Lottie, who was dead long before I was born, had a series of hand-painted Limoges bouillon cups, each one different, and little sterling bouillon spoons. I have them now, but never use them—I've never had a dozen people in for bouillon. Who were her guests, in her little town of eighteen hundred souls? No more do I use her four-yard-long damask tablecloths.

By the end of the nineteenth century, small villages like Watseka and Chenoa and Bloomfield, Illinois, had grown, though not much, and had come to have a certain imposing stability, with big Victorian houses and wide streets shaded by elms—the beautiful elms now all gone, killed by Dutch elm disease decades ago—and horse chestnut trees. If at first the houses were mere sheds and cabins, most of the houses in Watseka came to have gingerbread eaves and porch swings, and hollyhocks in the back-yards; one house, even now, like the name of the owners (the L'Angeliers), was an antebellum misfit with two-story plantation columns instead of the usual front porch. In Luann Landon's charming *Dinner at Miss Lady's* I learn that the food—biscuits and pies—was similar in small-town Illinois and small-town Georgia. We don't see those sour pie cherries anymore, nor the black raspberries and black walnuts we used to have.

These days in Watseka, Illinois, population 5,255, there's a Mexican restaurant and a pizza joint; some of the houses have been torn down for banks and drive-ins, or the odd double-wide installed right next to an old, dignified white Queen Anne. There are eighteen churches, two of them Catholic. There are Jehovah's

Witnesses, Mormons, and one, Trinity Church, whose Web site comes up in Chinese as well as English. You can buy a teeny house for $25,000 in Watseka, or a lovely big old one for $150,000.

Chenoa, Illinois, has 1,785 folks. The ethnic makeup of the town is still mostly white, European, often German, according to the census; fewer than 1 percent are African Americans, even fewer Native Americans, who were run off nearly two centuries ago for the valuable farmland. Chenoa is now around 5 percent Hispanic, a population that grew from 2 percent since the last census. The constituents are Republicans almost universally, with an increasing Tea Party presence, though "the Watseka Tea Party does not want to be part of the GOP," says its local spokesman. "The establishment is not something we're interested in, in its current form." They say they think the present GOP is too obstructionist and not enough interested in "doing what's right."

29

Rich in Uncles

In the Victorian midwestern fashion, families were large well into the twentieth century. I was a child rich in uncles. Each of my parents was the youngest in a big family, and between them they had fourteen siblings. Most of these married, giving us thirty aunts and uncles, counting remarriages and not counting the honorary uncles—adult friends of my parents whom we called uncle. Do people have uncles anymore? Were uncles, nowadays represented as pedophiles and sadists, just another regretted part of a past world of genial relatives and unquestioned commitments, a boon not to be recovered?

Do men think of themselves as uncles now, in the serious, responsible way that unclehood used to imply? Catharine's uncles counseled her and guarded her virtue. My uncles taught me long words, and started me out with a Brownie camera, brought me dolls and books. I treasure an amethyst from my uncle Tom, sent from India during the Second World War, and a ring from Uncle Bill, cut down from one of his rings. The point is, though, that I owe my uncles far more than material things—a sympathy for men, for one thing, and the ability to see their point of view, trapped in their difficult lives.

How many times did I let my uncle Bill down? Now it seems a hundred times, when I could have driven up to see him, a lonely widower in his Ukiah motel, or picked up the phone. There is a moment when life reverses its notions of custody and responsibility, and puts you in charge of your parents, though I hadn't understood this as it was happening. There was my uncle Bill's ulcer and my uncle Ed's diabetes. I worried about my uncles, I felt them to be more vulnerable than I.

My brother and I were the objects of much kindness, I think, because our numerous aunts and uncles had produced few children of their own. I've been told that not reproducing is a common reaction to having been part of a big family. With so few nieces and nephews special curiosity was focused on me, the first child to be born to the youngest siblings, Frances and Dolph, when they were thirty and forty years old.

My Watseka aunts on my mother's side were Grace, Martha, and Henrietta, in order of age and degree of stoutness, with Aunt Grace the fattest, a farm lady with a robust appetite. Aunt Grace's dinners were huge plates of fried chicken and several forms of potato, white, sweet, hash brown, and mashed. My father's sisters were Lucy, Helen, Mabel, Ruth, and Pearl. Aunts by marriage added Ruby, Opal, and Goldie to this jewel box of female relatives, and there were also Lola, who may not have actually been married to my rascal uncle Jack, and perhaps an aunt called Fern, married to my bachelor uncle Charlie late in life, whom I didn't really know. Nor did I ever meet Aunt Lucy, my father's oldest sister, confined since her teens, back in the 1880s, to a mental institution. Aunt Lucy appears in some early family photos, and she does have, when you come to look at her, an odd, mad expression on what is otherwise a recognizable Lain face, strong-jawed, with the high forehead. My brother and I had never heard of her until 1950 or so, when my father got a phone call, within our hearing, telling him she had died at last. "Oh, Lucy's gone, then, well . . .," he was saying. We drew nearer to listen.

Now, I realize, now that there's no one to ask, that I know little

about the girlhoods and early lives of my aunts. I used to worry
about Aunt Henrietta, who referred to herself as an "old maid."
Since I had always understood that women grew up and got married, it puzzled me that she had not. In fact, she always seemed
cheerful, and I have since read that among human categories, the
unhappiest are unmarried men, but the happiest are unmarried
women.

Uncle Lester was a banker and a gruff, emphatic man with
scary eyes magnified by his thick cataract-corrective lenses. The
family tale was told that he was beloved in Chenoa because when
the banks failed in the Depression, he didn't foreclose on anyone.
These were all mild, principled, affable people, accepting of other
people's foibles, not expecting much excitement in their lives. For
anything to happen, you had to go to iniquitous and anomic Chicago.

There was quite a pool of uncles I didn't know very well. On
my mother's side—the Elder side—I had the terrifying beetle-
browed uncle Stanley Lee in his denim overalls coming in from
the fields to scrunch my hand in his strong callused one and say,
"That's a girl, a grip like her dad's." His fascination for me was
that he was supposedly descended from Light Horse Harry Lee,
the Revolutionary War figure, a Virginian—a Southerner—and
here we were in the Land of Lincoln, resolutely Yankee.

Uncle Stanley and Uncle Lester—Unkie Unc—were uncles
by marriage, and then there were my mother's real brothers, Tom
and Ed Elder, the latter my favorite uncle. Even as a tiny child, I
think I felt not stronger than they but worried about my uncles.
They seemed vulnerable and too docile to get along in a man's
life. I suppose men often strike women this way; it may even be
that they employ a sort of unconscious strategy to profit from

female solicitude. In any case, my sweetest uncle, of whom I felt the most protective, was my uncle Ed Elder. Children do worry about adults and wonder if they are happy. From a child's perspective he was an adult, but looking back, I see he must have been small for a man, five feet four or five, and plump and bald— plump at least till he became ill. Uncle Ed was a bachelor, and lived with my spinster aunt.

The Elder family parade

Aunt Bappy kept house for Uncle Ed in the Victorian house the two of them had been raised in, in Watseka, a big, white clapboard house with an iron stove and a drying rack that pulled up to the kitchen ceiling. Earlier, before I can remember, both Aunt Henrietta and Aunt Martha had lived there, but at some point Aunt Martha had been seconded to Chenoa to nurse dying Great-aunt Lottie—her aunt. Midwestern women born in the last decade of the nineteenth century, like people centuries earlier, were greatly occupied with nursing the sick—relatives, dependents, friends. Even in my childhood in the 1940s, several school friends were bedridden with rheumatic fever and had to stay home for a year. How we envied those lucky children!

Aunt Martha's story was, after Great-aunt Lottie died, she married Lottie's husband, Uncle Lester, making him my double uncle. For a man to marry his dead wife's sister was legally forbidden in the nineteenth century, in England at least, and only permitted there in 1907. I don't know about a dead wife's niece.

Uncle Ed worked in a drugstore their father had owned. Once I heard the disapproving neighbor Mrs. Weatherwax say, "Eddie Elder was never very interested in school." I have a picture of him as a child in his sailor blouse, with his deep, beautiful, hopeful little boy's gaze, never dreaming he needed to be good in school, or that he'd be going off to the First World War, him so small, and France so far—though I suppose he didn't feel as small there. I loved him very much. He had hobbies that he would share with me, and things he had brought back from the war, and magazines like *Esquire, Collier's, The Saturday Evening Post,* and *National Geographic.* I was amazed by the Petty and Vargas girls in *Esquire.* He had his fountain pens, his particular leather easy chair, and lots of cameras. His pens came down to me when he died, and I still write with them.

Now I see that there must have been a hollow in his life— could he have been gay? Of course that didn't occur to me in those days, nor did I ever hear it hinted at, nor would I have known what they were talking about. Did he just think himself too poor and small to marry? Was he poor? How would I know?

The great adventure of his life must have been as a soldier in the First World War, when he sent home to his sisters little satin purses and aprons embroidered "Bienvenue en France."

When he died, in his fifties, they found a letter in his wallet from me, a six-year-old's clumsy writing, not about anything in particular. I worried that it wouldn't have meant anything to him at all if there had been much else in his life. Slyly, Aunt Opal hinted of rumors that when he went out with the boys, he got too drunk to pay for his round.

Uncle Ed died in his fifties from "not taking care of himself," Mrs. Weatherwax's diagnosis. His was my first loss to death and I took it bitterly. Of course we're all uneasy with death, how could we not be? In some way I felt that I didn't take good enough care of him, of any of them, and now they are all dead. Then, I had excuses—I was not old enough, or I was too busy with my little children—but sins of omission are always hardest to bear; we can have more rationalizations about the sins we commit on purpose.

Of course I don't know what went on in their hearts, or how they amused themselves. There were no operas or nightclubs in their towns; did they miss them? Do expectations dampen down to the level of possibilities? Anyway, there is plenty of amusement in gossip—my aunts chuckling over their quilt patching as they reminisce: "Remember the time druggist Ray found the baby on his doorstep?" Or "How about the way Mrs. Stone and Mr. Affleck pulled out of their driveways at the same peculiar times of day, thinking nobody noticed?"

Gossip implies an engagement with others, an interest in them, a sense of narrative, and pleasure in stories well told. They weren't judgmental. In fact, I suspected an inner seditiousness that slightly belied their perfect compliance with local customs.

Once, as an adolescent, when asked if I was ready for church, I said defiantly, "I'm not going. I wouldn't know how to behave," which made them laugh approvingly, commending me for principles, and go off without me, though I had expected censure.

The only censoriousness I can remember was directed at their sisterinlaw, poor Aunt Opal, who married my uncle Tom, to the consternation of his sisters Frances, Martha, Henrietta, and Grace, who had learned she had once been a hairdresser. Especially for my aunts Henrietta, Martha, and Grace, Aunt Opal could do no right. Whatever she wore or served to eat was mocked, and they believed her to be unkind to their beloved brother Tom. I always felt defensive of kindly, pretty Aunt Opal, who taught me things like how to fan out the silverware on a buffet table (she had once worked in catering); but I admit I became a little snobbish too, when I was old enough to notice the 3D hologram of Leonardo da Vinci's *The Last Supper* hanging in her living room. I took it as a personal humiliation that such an error of taste could arise in my family, whose walls otherwise were hung with slightly amateurish oil paintings and watercolors by grandmothers and aunts—refinements the women in the family thought important.

30

Summer

The climate of the Midwest is such that people try to escape it both in winter and in summer, which in my family meant a trek to upper Michigan in July. Today I can see on the map that St. Ignace, where we spent our childhood summers, is farther north than Montreal, which accounts for my recollection that to get there from central Illinois was a matter of an endless journey to a remote, primeval no-man's-land. Here my family had a log house, which had been built by my uncle Lester decades before, and here we would spend the months of summer, the pinnacle of my family's emphasis on bucolic self-reliance.

I felt for this house the special love that almost everyone, I've since discovered, feels for a summer house—a love quite different from the feelings you have for the house you grow up in. Perhaps a summer house is where, forced into your own company, you discover that you are yourself, and maybe that's something that can't happen in an ordinary life, when you belong to your parents and school. The organized city child is deprived of these hours of messing around alone, though they must be the crucial ones in which we discover things, develop a point of view, learn to rely on ourselves as reliable observers, establish in our own minds that we are we.

There's a bridge now, but in those days, you reached the northern shore of the Great Lakes by means of giant steam ferries across the isthmus that connects Lake Michigan to Lake Huron—the Straits of Mackinac. The very word *straits* must have added to our sense of the difficulty and adventure in getting there. The waters of this body were often rough, and sometimes the crossings would be canceled—today they are designated as a Shipwreck Preserve. The vessels I remember were the enormous *Chief Wawatam* and the *Sainte Marie*. When you embarked you couldn't see the opposite shore, and the deep call of the horns gave the sense of an ocean ahead, an ocean voyage at last.

My little brother and I would feel sick, excited fear, arriving early each summer, to see what natural disasters would have befallen the house during the winter. The snow of northern Michigan might have reached the eaves and pushed the windows in. Each spring the plaster chinks between the logs would have fallen out and have to be replaced by my father, who would also repaint the logs with creosote against termites, scenting our hair and clothes for days with piney stink. Screens were put up, the chimney cleaned. The winter would have washed things up on the shore in front of the house—sometimes logs, or corpses of fish quite strangely near the porch, suggesting how the icy waves had risen to strike the door of the empty house.

My parents thought that life in summer must be lived as simply as possible, to invoke a virtuous sense of rustication and closeness to nature. This is a conventional enough belief, maybe even a truth, and the origin of the belief that sending low-income kids to camp to live in uncomfortable tents in the country improves their chances in life. Whether my parents' theories were born to justify the discomforts of our cabin or the discomforts had fostered the theories I have no idea.

Certainly we had none of the ordinary amenities of wintertime in town—our cabin for years had no indoor plumbing and no running water except what you pumped in at the sink. We had an icebox and a weekly block of ice. We slept on a screened-in porch, or in a hot little room under the eaves, the windows open equally to lake breezes and mosquitoes. The peeled logs of the walls and pine floorboards under bare feet gave us splinters. We had electricity—a tiny bulb by the outhouse that attracted June bugs, so that a small child obliged to creep out there in the night would inevitably step on their crunchy corpses. (This outhouse was eventually deemed too spartan even for us, and indoor plumb-ing was installed.) We had kerosene lamps too, for when the elec-tricity failed, as it might in the black summer storms that swept across the Great Lakes, tossing up oceanic whitecaps.

The cabin, named Plawicki, kept my father busy chinking the logs, bringing the wood in, hammering loose shingles on the roof like a pioneer homesteader. I realize now what a lot of work our carefree life must have been for mother too, a demanding succes-sion of rituals to do with water gathering, fire tending, and

My playpen at Plawicki

protecting her young from wildlife, for in this part of the country there were bears, skunks, mosquitoes, spiders, bloodsuckers, porcupines, chiggers, snakes, wolves, and bats.

With some of these, we shared the house—a skunk once came to live under the floorboards, a problem delicate to resolve. The bats that wheeled out of hiding at dusk would by late evening have returned to their perches, disguised as folded leaves under the eaves of our sleeping porch. The leeches tried to fasten on to our thighs in the shallow water. The mosquitoes continued their whining circles overhead, and in the distance, the cries of coyotes or wolves.

Well, didn't we come from pioneer stock? My parents loved living the life of forebears—say, of Catharine and Eleazer, or Catharine's mother, Anne Perkins, who had written of being stranded in her cabin up on the Canadian border, left alone in a snowstorm, in labor, nearly two hundred years before. Though I hadn't read her memories of her frightening experience, giving birth in a snowbound cabin on the border of Canada, it had happened in a place very similar, only a few hundred miles to the east.

Though my parents evidently loved busying themselves with nesting and security, it was the sense of menace my brother and I loved. Personifications of summer in classical paintings suggest how enduring is the impression of this season as safe, garlanded, unclothed, carefree, and benign, but to us it seemed the opposite, a season of rather delicious peril. We had to be greased against mosquitoes and burrowing chiggers, pulled indoors when the bats began to swoop, warned against the mother bears that were sure to be lurking near the blueberries, be ever on the lookout for skunks and porcupines, against which we would need to protect our dog Tarby if not ourselves. How we dreaded the slimy leeches lurking in the shallow water—bloodsuckers waiting to attach themselves to our skinny legs. There were the constant dangers of polio and drowning. Even the scratchy berry brambles might hurt us, and down by the water, a malevolent skunk cabbage, entrapping poor insects to their sticky death, could get you with its odious scent if you happened to brush against it.

So of course we loved our summer house, with its danger and discomforts, more than we loved our "real" house, scene of schoolwork, regulation, orderly life. The philosopher Bachelard speaks of the way many of our ideas and recollections are attached to specific rooms and places to which we'll return all our lives. "The house is one of the greatest powers of integration for the thoughts, memories and dreams of mankind." He is talking about the primordial birth house, as a refuge and shelter, so his imagery is that of the winter house, which protects with warmth and light against the darkness and cold, both real and spiritual, of the world. "We comfort ourselves by reliving memories of protection." But the summer house is strangely the opposite, a house that forces us into the world on our own resources and thus reassures us about our strengths. It is not a shelter but a jumping-off place, benignly promising that our explorations and solitary wanderings won't bring us to grief, and that we'll be able to survive the more serious wintry perils later on.

There's a theory of memory that says that you remember more of the things that happen when you were happy than when you weren't. (There is another that says the opposite.) The happiness of our summer house was conveyed in the lightened mood of the adults, the warm sense of idleness, the growly voices of my father and his brothers playing pitch on the porch, the happy pastimes of fishing, swimming, berrying (wild strawberries if we got there early enough in June, and blueberries later in the summer).

All these things our family did together. But more important was the sense of being alone. If the summer house evokes a memory of ideal, it was because you were unsupervised, or felt yourself to be so. Turned loose to wander in the woods, we could be gone for hours without being reproached, or hole up some-where and read all day.

Reading is the solitary essential pastime to which all summer houses are peculiarly dedicated. You can read long classics or trash. In our cabin I read stories of other children's summers— *Five Little Peppers and How They Grew;* or *Diddie, Dumps and Tot,* a book now so politically incorrect, with its references to picka-ninnies, a bookseller once refused to sell it to me lest my own children read it; or horrible Elsie Dinsmore. Later I read the racy historical novels The Literary Guild sent to my mother.

Another luxury is not reading at all. It's the boredom of sum-mer that seems in retrospect the most precious and formative thing. The perfect summer house has to have deep corners and retreats to hide and dream in. In our cabin it was a mezzanine under the eaves that gave a view of the grown-ups downstairs. Sheets of heat wafted up from the fireplace. On hot days, the sun heating the creosote stifled with its smell of pitch and a dusty scent of the old curtains. Here I would make worlds of paper dolls, or weave on my Indian bead loom.

In the winter world of the real house, sober furniture is dedi-cated to its uses—you sit on an upholstered chair, eat at a mahog-any table—but a summer house is ruled by caprice. The furniture is made of birch logs and bark, the chandelier is made of coffee tins painted bronze by my great-aunt Lottie——the same decorative impulses that dictate the fanciful antler constructions of Adirondack houses. According to the whole summer house tradition, you pretend to some alien condition. In California, before the Second World War, my husband spent his summers on Catalina Island, there on the Pacific Rim where the fancy was to be Japanese. They had straw mats and screens and paper lanterns. In Michigan, it was to be an Indian, maybe in the same contrite, propitiatory spirit that hunters wear horns and pretend to be deer. We wore buckskin moccasins and had baskets everywhere.

As in Moline, in Michigan, Native Americans were foremost in our consciousness because they were featured in local legend and decor, with the sale of deerskin moccasins and tiny bark wigwams at tourist shops, and in the names of things. The Indians fishing near our cabin or stretched out along the pier in the village were fat and amiable and wore plaid shirts. We knew that Mr. Barker, a friend of our father's who ran a nearby lodge, was mostly Sioux. It seemed to my brother and me that our father was privileged to be taken fishing far into Canada with a real Indian, and we expected he'd come back with mysterious lore. We felt not sympathy but chagrin when once he nearly drowned, sinking in his waders like a city slicker. But he did learn somewhere to strip the bark from birch trees, and he made us a tepee, a little summer house of our own to hide away in.

At the end of summer, the rituals are of battening down, closing up. Back go the shutters, the rugs are rolled, the lawn chairs stacked on the porch under sheets of oilcloth and a piece of old sail. A whiff of winter appears in the space of a day, warning of snow and desolation. Ideas of school, new clothes, worldly winter notions, suddenly beguile. We hated to leave Plawicki alone, "left like a shell on a sandhill to fill with dry salt grains now that life had left it," as Virginia Woolf wrote of that time when the family goes away from the summer house, worried as to what will happen without them. Of course it isn't the house you really worry about so much as for yourselves, that you won't be back.

And one summer, we weren't. Something happened. Time passed, we grew, our aunts and uncles died, the house was sold. Since then I've had another house by a lake, but it isn't the same. Of course neither are we.

31

In God We Trusted . . .

Ranna Cossitt, who came to America, was either a Catholic who converted to Protestantism or a Protestant all along, debatable, just as there's some argument about whether America was founded as a Christian nation. The attitudes of people like Anne and her pious husband, John Perkins, underlay the somewhat reflex piety of Illinois during my childhood, but although for them religion involved a vivid daily brush with Satan and God, I doubt that my aunts and uncles thought too much about either figure. They probably believed in God; but for Anne and John, and for many, His existence was a matter of daily discussion.

In Moline somehow everyone knew everyone's religion, mostly Protestant. The Scandinavians were Lutheran, but those who weren't belonged to a variety of other Protestant denominations, among which the Congregational Church in our view predominated. The pretty church building had been endowed by John Deere himself and thus was somehow the correct place to worship, so that despite generations of Episcopalian forebears, my parents went there, or rather, sent my brother and me there to Sunday school. When you came out of our church, you could see to the left, down the street, the words "Jesus Saves" in neon on the side of another building that I believed to be a bank but was in fact another church, apparently of an evangelical nature, though no one we knew went to it and I never heard its name.

Our father and mother didn't go to church at all, or at least not very often, maybe at Easter and Christmas, and sometimes Mother's Day, when my mother wore a white flower to signify that her own mother was dead. I'd be wearing a pink one, signify ing a living mother—somewhat redundantly, for Mother was right there. Before we went in to find our pew, she would scrub my face with her hanky, which she had daintily moistened with spit. When I once challenged the fact that though my brother and I had to go to Sunday school, our parents didn't, they frostily explained that "religion is part of your education, like arithmetic or geography, and we had to go when we were children, for the same reason."

I didn't really mind—I liked Sunday school, and as a teenager taught the younger children, according to a prescribed syllabus that featured interesting Bible stories, always from the New Testa ment. When once as a younger child I was given a book of Bible stories from the Old Testament, I was outraged by the unfairness and wickedness portrayed in it, and by the way the person you liked least always triumphed, with the approval of God. Things were not very much better in the New Testament—for poor Martha, for instance—but they were better, and you couldn't re gret turning out the money changers and the fact that Judas was punished, unlike Abraham, who so richly deserved it. I thought Abraham ought to have accepted eternal damnation for the sake of his little boy, and couldn't respect his ideas of obedience and blind trust.

I don't think these qualities were particularly emphasized in our church either. When younger, I did have a period—of a few days only—of intense and morbid conviction of sin and death, and prayed, sobbing, to God. I was probably ten, and this fit of

metaphysical anxiety might have come with my first real intima-
tion of mortality. But in Sunday school we were not told much
about sin or hell, or anything else disturbing, only about goodness and service.

I am hardly the first person to have dismissed religion at the
sticking point when you first realize it prompts people to do what
they know is wrong; but I had an enthusiastic love of dressing up
in robes—I wore one when as an exemplary child I got to read
the lesson at the eleven o'clock service on Children's Day, or sang
in the choir—and I loved the stately language of the King James
prayers, the flags carried in the processional. (Our Congregational minister, the Reverend William Hodgson, was an Anglican
priest from England, and so was the liturgy. We liked to spin romantic stories about his flight from some crime committed over
there.) I loved the Christmas processional when we all got to sing
Gounod's "Lovely appear over the mountain / The feet of them
that preach, and bring good news of peace. . . ."

As far as I knew, there were two Jews in our school—Sherwin
Brotman and Gary Cohen. Sherwin was handsome, and Gary
had a blue Studebaker convertible, so each had his allure.
Our mothers wouldn't have wanted us to marry either of
these boys, but they worried most that we would marry Catholics,
and be condemned to lives of thankless childbearing and female
servitude. As it happened, there weren't many Catholics in our
school for our mothers to worry about—they went to a Catholic
school; and anyway, most lived across the river in Davenport,
Iowa. Marriage, in any case, was only for After College, and there
was no alternative to college; you went.

It's strange, given the resolute anti-Catholicism of some small
Illinois towns, that Catholics are now the single largest religious

group in Illinois, nearly a third of the population. They are a majority on the national Supreme Court, which would have panicked my mother and her friends. Their opposition was not based on theology, only on the attitude of the Church to contraception. Contraception was a blessing for their flapper generation, as their own mothers had borne endless children—my two grandmothers had sixteen living children between them, without counting miscarriages or stillbirths, which aren't recorded, and they doubtless had had plenty to say about the woman's lot, and suffused their daughters' hearts with gratitude for the arrival of Family Planning.

It was a shock to my brother and me, when I was twelve or so, and an event surrounded by mystery—our father resigned or was fired from his job as the high school principal and took another that required him to drive off to Missouri on Monday mornings and come home on Thursday nights. In Missouri, he visited colleges, and apparently played lots of golf too, and gin rummy, exploits involving winnings, which he would recount when he got home, but what he actually did was less clear.

The explanation in my family for this sudden career change I was eventually to learn; whether or not there was another side of it I never did find out. Following an incident of plagiarism by a schoolboard member's daughter, my father insisted that a literary prize she had been given be withdrawn. In the resulting impasse between him and the school board, he was offered a choice between being fired with ten thousand dollars or being promoted to the presidency of a junior college then being organized, but without the money. He took the ten thousand and another job, in "audiovisual education," which meant working with colleges setting up film libraries and running film rentals—a sort of proto-Blockbuster; beyond that, we didn't know what he did. He was soon promoted.

His new company proposed that we move to the larger and more significant region—Texas. This thrilling possibility transformed my life for a few weeks. I announced it to my friends, was feted and bidden good-bye, and given a bracelet I still have, engraved with love from "the gang."

Then my father, who had gone down there to find a house, came back and said, "I don't think we can possibly live in a place like that." He didn't really explain why, but we could imagine: cowboys, cactus, six-shooters, no golf. Just like that, "we are not moving." The humiliation was almost too much for me. Not moving to Texas, the best chance of the great world I'd had till then, brought on the worst fit of misery and histrionic despair I had ever had up till then.

The Dark Shadow

On Saturdays, kids went to the movies: Roy Rogers, Hopalong Cassidy, the Cisco Kid, double features. Our moms dropped us off; we could walk downtown to the Orpheum when we were older, but not when we were eleven. Besides the features, there were newsreels and cartoons. Throughout the war, these featured indistinct images of explosions, marching, and formations of planes taking off to go save democracy. The familiar voice of *The March of Time* was almost reassuring, no matter what the sight.

One particular day in spring 1945, the newsreels showed something our mothers would not have let us see, and if the theater had posted a warning that you might not like your child to see this, our mothers didn't know about it. Stick-figure humans tottering toward the camera with feeble, waving arms, or lying emaciated on bunks; and other images of dead people stacked up, and soldiers helping the dying. Skeleton people, strangely white against the sordid darkness of their prison, in rags, yet smiling. Even the ones lying down would stir their heads and grin. Visions of the skeleton people and the stacked-up dead people would never leave me, and to this day they are before me.

We knew we couldn't tell our parents about the terrible thing we had seen. For one thing, they wouldn't let us go to the movies anymore if they knew. But mainly we wanted to spare them, hoping they would never hear about these murders that had happened far away.

Flyover

My father cherished the wish that I'd grow up to be an airline stewardess. He thought that would be the perfect job for a girl—you got to travel, would meet eligible men among whom to choose a husband, and, having seen the world, would settle down with less restiveness than he perceived already to exist in me. The catch was that you had to be at least five feet four, and it early became plain that I wasn't going to make it.

I too wanted to be a stewardess. Back then, in the forties and fifties, "stewies" were regarded as glamorous globetrotters, and to pass the time between college and marriage, seeing the world was to my mind highly preferable to the alternatives that society presented, at least in downstate Illinois: secretary, schoolteacher, or nurse—three professions I had resolved from the time I was a child never ever to touch. For then I would be like my mother and her friends and all the other women in Moline, Illinois, and I was not going to be like them, even though I had no better plan in mind. It was not that I didn't love and admire them, it was that I could see that their lives were orderly and unsurprising.

But I'd have to grow to be five feet four or five. From kindergarten on I was the smallest girl in my class. Family concern had been directed at my smallness from my infancy, when the ironing lady is said to have told my mother, "You'll never raise her." My preschool puniness and indifference to eating had induced Dr. Arp to prescribe "cordial"—a hated tablespoon of muscatel before dinner, poured from a jug stored in the garage to keep it cold. No eagerly attended growth spurt, no frantic vitamin regime, had the slightest effect on my fate: to be small like my mother, my aunts, and even Mother's brothers, my uncles. My father at six feet towered over us.

How anxiously I examined growth charts and stood myself against the five-foot mark on the scale at the school gym. With my destiny depending on my size, I had little patience with people who pointed out the advantages of being "petite." Chiefly these were that boys liked you, especially then, before their growth spurts, and that your shoes were so cute and little. (The Moline Swedish girls were all destined to be tall, beautiful blondes with large feet.)

I would grow to be five feet one. That is, petite. The phenomenology of smallness: your character is formed by whether you dominate your surroundings in size or must accommodate to them and learn watchful habits, like a child. The tall must stoop under branches and tuck up their limbs in theater seats. On walks with my husband (who is six feet four), we see different parts of the world—he sees birds in trees, and I the low-growing wildflowers or interesting rocks. Our ideas of shelves are different. To look at things less optimistically, does a small person develop traits of devious cleverness to atone for her lack of brute force? At least this is what men have always said of women in general.

And being treated like a child has its corollary; I have to admit that I am still somewhat infantilized by these attentions and myself reach for someone's hand if they don't take mine, expecting protection and care. Do you keep a childlike perspective? Maybe. As the child watches with her own form of

detachment the actions of the adult world, she develops a judgmental, observant habit of mind. Perhaps it isn't coincidental
that women writers are often small.

Have you ever felt the oddness of realizing that some clear
memory was registered in your consciousness at a time when
someone looking at you would have seen a child three feet high,
and that though you were looking out of your eyes from somewhere around your parents' knees, this memory fits neatly into
your scheme of things as if you'd experienced it with your adult
self? For instance, I remember as if it were yesterday, in the
phrase, being lost at the Indian powwow—not being scared, but
being humiliated, to hear on the loudspeaker, over the tom-
toms, the voice asking people to look for the lost child Diane
Lain and take her to the podium, where her parents were frantic. I was five, and hadn't realized, or yet realized, I was lost. I
was free. Maybe this was where I got a taste for freedom, and
the fear of it too.

As I look back to when I was in my teens, dating in Moline
seems like something from the TV series *Happy Days,* affirming
all the clichés about that optimistic and innocent period, and in
some ways it wasn't greatly changed from the 1790s. I went to
teen activities at church, went to movies and dances, sometimes
daringly to roadhouses where you drank too much—probably
not an option in the eighteenth century—necked a little in the
car, with the usual first-base, second-base strictures. Your big
worries were your date, your prom dress, and whether the cor-
sage would match and be the right flower. Orchids were hoped
for, but most likely you'd get carnations or gardenias.

You worried about who would ask you to the prom, of course,

and above all that the right person would ask in time, because our mothers enforced the rule that you had to stick with the person you accepted first, even if a preferred person asked you afterward. In practice, this fear was eliminated by going steady; I had a steady boyfriend, a nondramatic and pleasant young man who expected to inherit a beer distribution company.

I wasn't interested in boys really then, and couldn't understand how girls could Get into Trouble, when the penalty of possible pregnancy was so dire—marriage, unless the boy joined the navy, and in that case unwed motherhood. What you did about that final disgrace, I didn't know. My mother told me years later that she and her friends had a list of cooperative doctors, in case, but she needn't have worried about me—my hormones were indolent, my mind on higher things.

However, once you got your period, there was the ritual equivalent of female circumcision: the Tampax initiation. Informed older girls (aged fourteen or so) would break the news that you needn't use horrible, soggy, and unreliable Kotex pads, as proposed by mothers and school nurses; tampons were much better. These were said not to impede virginity—the hymen was elastic and resilient, if we even had hymens, owing to bike accidents and horseback riding. Anyway, we didn't care if our hymens got broken, it didn't seem the business of some male; we resisted the requirement of virginity on nascent feminist principles, though we didn't plan on losing it either.

The only impediment with Tampax was not being sure you really had an opening or where on earth it was, and it required a lot of coaching from other girls, plus a mirror and standing with one leg on a stool, shaking with effort and nervousness.

34

Mademoiselle

When I was seventeen, I went off to Stephens College, a women's college in Missouri selected by my parents. My father had met the dean and admired his theories of female education. I still have no idea why I was so uninvolved in choosing a college for myself; I think, though, it was because I was unable to imagine leaving home, for it turned out that despite my earnest, abiding wish to escape from Moline, at this first attempt, I was miserably homesick. My parents, alarmed by my sobbing phone calls, dispatched my father to drive to Missouri to explain that of course a beloved daughter could come home anytime. But then, having failed at going away, I would have to live in my old room and perhaps work in an office; life would go on along another track. This drab alternative brought me to a sense of what was at stake.

Stephens added greatly to my education in a number of ways; above all it gave me a little bit of intellectual self-confidence, one of the hopes on which the curriculum was based. It had a philosophy of women's education holding that girls should know about music and art (Humanities class) and have a basic understanding of consumer economics. It was mindful, in the world of female education, that we would also be getting married—no alternative was envisaged. So some effort was made to enhance our marketability—each student received a hair and makeup consultation by the resident hairdresser, Mr. Detchmendy. You always knew when someone had just had her appointment; for about a week afterward she'd be luridly enhanced with eye shadow and mascara, hair parted unfamiliarly, wearing a new shade of lipstick.

But we were also to be educated to be stimulating intellectual companions for our rising husbands, and mothers of successful children—we were required to take Marriage and the Family. I secretly appreciated such information as that the penis is actually very clean, more often washed, in fact than parts of

During my stint at Mademoiselle

our own anatomy that are more secluded. We knew such classes were an improvement on the earlier idea that girls didn't need much education at all, or only education classes that would fit you to be a teacher until you got married.

There was a regional element to this philosophy. Women my same age in eastern colleges were certainly getting a serious education at Smith or Radcliffe with a view to having professions; but this program hadn't yet come to the Midwest, or at least not to our circles. Airline stewardess, secretary, teacher, nurse—that was it. So, eager to avoid these fates, when I was nineteen, just finishing my sophomore year, at the urging of my English teacher, Mr. Charles Madden, I went for the first time east of the Mississippi (except that Moline actually lies on its east bank): to New York.

In high school, Miss Barbara Garst was the teacher whose encouragement was important to me—a plump, dynamic spinster with a gravelly voice who went on to be a "teacher of the year," involving a sabbatical to England, where she made friends with some important English literary figures, like Karl Miller, the editor of the *New Statesman,* who, when I met him years later, told of stopping in our town, Moline, Illinois, to visit her— the only reported instance of the conjunction of our town with the distant literary world, except for the grave of one of Charles Dickens's children, Frank, in our local cemetery. Frank was a grown man, a Canadian Mountie, adventuring far from England, but I had imagined him as a poor little boy, as unlucky as I, to have strayed into our benighted town.

Despite her trip to England, Miss Garst had not suggested that the outside world would be discoverable by her students; but

I was lucky with Stephens, which had small classes so that some
teachers took an interest in me; in particular, Mr. Madden, like
Miss Garst, who praised my stories and read them aloud, and encouraged me to enter a contest in a periodical that existed then—
Mademoiselle magazine. I won a place in the contest, and would be
one of twenty girls working for *Mademoiselle* for a month in the
summer. I was very excited by the prospect of this adventure, and
a little frightened, and, much to my surprise, daunted.

This was the summer, 1953, subsequently immortalized by
Sylvia Plath in her novel *The Bell Jar,* with vivid images of the
twenty girl guest editors throwing up en masse in the women's
bathroom of the Barbizon Hotel, poisoned by crab salad from the
test kitchen of BBDO, an advertising agency. I was less sick than
some others, because I had never eaten crab and was suspicious of
it, an ingredient that had never come to Moline, as far as I knew.

I went to New York directly from college, instead of going back
to Oregon, where my parents now lived; my father had been trans-
ferred to a place, in our view, much pleasanter than Texas. I was
planning to get married later in the summer, but was perfectly
content to leave the details to my mother, a sign, in retrospect, that
I must have had misgivings about marriage, the way I had had
about college. But if I did, I wasn't aware of them—everyone was
getting married, it was what you did, preferably before you had
graduated. I see now that I wasn't deeply interested in weddings
per se either—I was much more interested in New York.

I took with me much advice, some clothes chosen according
to instructions from the magazine—dark colors, sleeves—and I
would need hats and gloves. And in case of difficulties, I was
given the addresses of certain acquaintances of my relatives, in

particular my uncle Bill's friend Mr. Herbert Solomon, met in the course of Uncle Bill's annual buying trips to New York. I was more or less unaware of the family concern that went with me on this trip, but I see now my inexperience, whatever character defects they spotted in me, and general cluelessness worried the whole family. They were all pleased that, assuming I came through, I would be safely marrying a promising medical student from a respectable family later in the summer; they feared that the big city would waylay me in some way.

It easily could have. There were parties, fashion shows, good-looking young men rustled up by the editors to escort us, new friends among the other guest editors. There was the general allure of the big city and the specific amusements of nightlife, which had not been available in Columbia, Missouri, or, needless to say, Moline, Illinois. I took to it, but profited only up to a point from the advice that had been so profusely elaborated for me. I allowed men to pick me up in respectable surroundings, like the Museum of Modern Art or the Metropolitan, and accepted lunches and drinks, but went no further. When, necking with a handsome advertising man—for this was the period so accurately described in the current television series *Mad Men*—I was asked whether I was a virgin, I was prompt with the answer that had served me well: yes, of course. I had learned from my college roommate Irby, from Savannah, that this was always the correct answer; the reply should be the same whatever the case. She had explained it: "In Georgia, everybody is a virgin." I also saw that in New York no one would have admitted to being a virgin; and I learned quite a bit else, all of it puzzling, about the worlds of fashion and publishing.

A memorable person who was kind to me that summer in

New York was the small, elderly, courtly Mr. Solomon. I think Uncle Bill had asked him to keep an eye on me, but he did it discreetly, by taking me to lunch a time or two, and introducing me to the world of beautiful clothes. This expanded my life, though maybe I would have caught on by myself to the interest of expensive dresses, design, and fashion (though of course I'd designed for my paper dolls). He explained with great tact that his wife had recently died, and he wondered whether I would accept one or two new things she had just bought and that would probably fit me. These were a black princess-style winter coat with a velvet collar from Best & Co. and a blue wool suit by Claire McCardell, elegant and expensive, that fitted me perfectly.

Until then, most of my clothes had been sewn by my mother, or by me. But although my mother sewed well and precisely, and had taken a tailoring class (and taught me), she did not put small covered weights in the hems of coats or line the skirts. In my mind, nothing could equal the glamour and utility of that suit, that coat, worn for years, by me and then my daughters. Both garments lived in the back of the closet in off years when shoulder pads were in, or out, or when hemlines changed, and had an extended life in the dress-up box for a decade after.

The month in New York was my first meeting with a literary world where people lived by writing, and were serious, even fierce, about it, Sylvia Plath above all. She was Literature up a notch from anything that had occurred to me. None of us could fail to notice the reverent way she was treated by the editors. She did not confide in most of us her anguish over the Rosenbergs, who were executed that summer, or her anguish in general, but instead wore a merry face and a perfect pageboy bob. We all had surrogate editorial assignments, shadowing the "real" editor. Sylvia was, as I

remember, the literary editor. I was "Health and Beauty," relegated to answering letters from *Mademoiselle* readers worrying
about makeup issues and blemishes.

The real editors took us to visit the now-legendary Leo Lerman
in his picturesque apartment stuffed with memorabilia and objects, and it was whispered that he was "queer," or "a fairy," whatever that actually entailed, the first I'd heard of homosexuality. All
in all, I was an unusually retarded, provincial nineteen-year-old
who found it scary in New York, especially the gravelly-voiced
women editors, who smoked and looked at the world through nar-
rowed eyes, so unlike the moms of Moline, though the moms too
smoked like fiends.

Faced with the challenges of the exotic world, my dreams of
adventure shriveled. I was not up to adventure. With two more
years of college to go, and with unexpressed misgivings, I went
ahead and married my boyfriend as scheduled and moved to California and planned to finish my education sometime later, a de-
ferment common for girls in those days. I had escaped from
Moline for college in a small town almost like Moline, and again
for a scary trip to New York, but I hadn't really escaped, and now
was in another predicament.

California

It was in California that I knew I had indeed finally left, or been cast out of, my native land—out of Moline and the Midwest. In Los Angeles I was fully deracinated; after this it wouldn't matter where I lived—England, France, Iran. Deracination was what I had always hoped for, but at first I didn't take to it. Here was a foreign landscape, foreign food, places on a different scale, and no one to talk to. I didn't thrive. I was still in America, banal and confining, or so I found it. I lost weight on my own bride cooking.

In those days, young women worked their husbands' way through graduate school. All the other secretaries and librarians I met at the UCLA library, where I got a job as a typist-clerk, were doing the same thing. I wasn't fitted for anything else—not even typing, really, though I had managed to pass the test; I was put to registering the receipt of the periodicals that came into the library in the periodical catalog, a job so boring I couldn't do it very well, and spent my time inventing useful errands or hopeful innovations, like poster painting or picking up supplies, and being beastly to another new employee, a kind and friendly but somehow abject middle-aged woman named Birdie.

Something about Birdie brought out all the worst tendencies to bullying and condescension in my character. I tried to reform when I overheard our supervisor, Miss Norton, reassuring Birdie to pay no attention to my behavior, that I was only a spoiled women's-college type she hadn't wanted to hire. I was shocked to be dismissed as a member of a category. If you grow up in a small

community, you are you. At its most impersonal you might be
"the Lain girl," or maybe "tenth grader at Coolidge," but never a
type, and an odious one at that.

This was my first real job, and I hated it with deep, existential
outrage. Going to work was a shocking lesson in reality everybody
experiences, the one that shows you where you are in the great
scheme of things and convinces you that you'd better get out of it
somehow. I was not the first young woman to find Motherhood to
be one way out.

I think Mary McCarthy says in one of her memoirs that it is
common for women writers to marry young, they want to get on
with things. Anyhow, if so, I was in that tradition, a teenager, but
I was surprised to find myself, within six years, the mother of
four little children. Unlike some of my friends, as a little girl, I
had never imagined future children or invented names for them;
they formed no part of my life plan, if I could be said to have had
one. I was simply me, an independent agent of perception blithely
stealing through existence with a kind of trustful enjoyment, like
an invisible, yet feeling, disembodied pair of eyes.

My first two babies were born within one calendar year. Irish
twins, people would smirk. I was overcome, at sea, victim of hy-
pochondria and sweating fits of anxiety. Perhaps this was partly
classic postpartum depression, a consequence of hormones reor-
ganizing themselves, but that was a condition unknown then. I
mention this for the pleasure of thinking again of the Tallmans.
Dr. Frank F. Tallman was a psychiatrist friend of my in-laws, I
think the chairman of the psychiatry department at the UCLA
medical school, where my husband was studying. For a long time
I couldn't think of Dr. and Mrs. Tallman without literally breaking
into sobs at their goodness. Their goodness consisted of offering

to babysit my children for a couple of hours once a week so I could go off and mess around.

In those days, the fifties, no one, myself included, acknowledged that babies were anything but a totally absorbing joy, so for someone to recognize that mothers need some time off—now a cliché of self-realization, unknown then—struck me as an overwhelmingly generous bolt from heaven. That someone understood that there might be more to me than a baby minder, that I might have an intellectual or artistic life, helped me understand this too. Without it, with only role models of selfless maternity on whom to pattern myself, I would surely have dissipated whatever abilities I might have had into the PTA and vague, or even acute, discontentedness or misery. I did have a taste of this kind of female activity by being president of a group formed of house staff and medical students' wives. This again brought out my tendency to bully and condescend—having discovered French food, I derided the tuna casserole recipes that were submitted to our cookbook project by a few benighted young wives, and refused to include things made with canned soup (still a staple of midwestern recipes). Like many another young housewife of the time, I had discovered *The* Gourmet *Cookbook*, and sedulously followed it into the culinary Brave New World, where I would meet Julia Child.

Eventually, I came to be delighted with motherhood too, but it was not an instantaneous emotion; it was more like what Alice Adams's mother told her about sexual intercourse: "eventually, it will thrill you."

36

Writer

I guess the impulse to write is inextinguishable, motherhood not‑withstanding, so when I got things in hand a bit, I began to look for writing jobs. For instance, a friend (Aljean Harmetz, the *New York Times* writer) and I wrote an episode for *My Three Sons*, a television series; and another friend, the future novelist Alison Lurie, also a young faculty wife, and I got research assistant jobs writing for UCLA professors. Little by little, we made their pa‑pers more amusing and coherent. They were amazed at what young housewives could do.

As a little girl in Moline, I didn't expect to be a writer, because I didn't know a writer was something you could be; I had no sense that books were still being written. I somehow supposed the books on our bookshelves at home, except for The Literary Guild vol‑umes delivered each month to my mother, had been written in a departed age, and the same was true of the books at school, where our English teacher, Miss Barbara Garst, prepared us to expect objections, on the grounds of raciness, from the school board when she boldly assigned us *Tom Jones*, an eighteenth‑century novel that hardly seems daring now. We also read books from the nineteenth century, like Dickens; my impression was that all books had been written already, mostly in the nineteenth century, except for a few, by John Steinbeck and Erskine Caldwell—*God's Little Acre* having been furtively handed around my seventh‑grade class.

Looking at that work now, I can't guess which of the passages could have so shocked and interested us. When I went to college, since I had barely read a book written in the twentieth century, I was thrilled by *The Naked and the Dead*, and *From Here to Eternity*, and Dos Passos's *U.S.A.*, with its scofflaw attitude to capital letters and spelling.

Now a grown-up would-be novelist, during the children's naps, I worked on a novel, my "real" writing. I was far from being like the driven and dedicated artists I so admired—like Sylvia Plath, for instance. The world didn't take my efforts very seriously, and I lacked the confidence to do so myself. I couldn't have filled in an "occupation" blank with any answer as pretentious—so it seemed— as "writer."

As I have said, this was still the period when women were encouraged to be educated, bright, and informed, but only in order to be better, more contented and effective, wives and mothers. Years later, finally reading *The Feminine Mystique*, I discovered that I had been to the very college, and taken the very class (Marriage and the Family), that Betty Friedan had chosen to exemplify the condition, so outwardly progressive, so actually confining, that she was denouncing. To be fair, I should add that though my first father-in-law, Lamar Johnson, was a pioneer of this philosophy of women's education, he was one of my main encouragers as I floundered in the mysteries and cares of motherhood, by urging me to have faith in my writing.

I don't know that he envisaged my having a career, though. It was Alison, an East Coast person who was soon to be a published novelist, who encouraged me to actually submit my work to a real publisher. She is a lifelong friend whom I still rely on for frank literary advice. And wardrobe counsel too: the only person who will say, "Dinny, I don't think you really see that blouse anymore. Throw it out."

It took me a long time, constrained by some lack of confidence, to define myself as a novelist, and I still leave my occupation blank on landing cards and other forms. No one has ever
questioned that a woman might not have any occupation worth
mentioning, bringing to mind the famous anecdote recounted by
Shirley Jackson about when, going into the hospital to have a
baby, she put "writer" on her admissions form only to see the
nurse cross that out and put "housewife."

I could add that, as for other mothers of large families (with
my stepchildren, we have seven children), art is caught on the fly,
in stolen moments of seclusion. How I dreamed of a reverent family tiptoeing to the closed door of my workroom with lunch and
dinner—the kind of luxurious pampering one gets from Bellagio
or Yaddo. But in fact I always tried not to mention my writing,
now not out of diffidence but because the testimony of many writers' families—usually male writers—convinced me it wasn't good
for children to have a writer parent. My husband, John Murray,
however, is supportive and solicitous to the perfect degree. Writers do need encouragement; we droop without it.

Here I'm just talking about the practical side of the Writing
Life, and little about the inner life, the way it feels to be a novelist, and how it shapes the way you see things. I suppose writers
are all different, but there are common threads to a writerly way
of making sense of the experience of living and needing to testify
to what you make of it. As time goes on, I've come to respect the
dictates of the unconscious, a buried artistic mind that seems to
operate best in the moments between sleep and waking, to sup-
ply ideas and details, and even phrases. If before going to sleep
you put a question to yourself—"What should Lulu do about
Amid?" for instance—the answer will often be there in the

morning, not dreamy, surreal passages but concrete artistic deci-
sions that often elude the conscious mind. Other writers—maybe
all writers—have reported this experience, as do chess players,
and woodcarvers and scientists. And if there's too much disagree-
ment between your conscious aims and your inner reservations,
the conflict can bring your novel to a halt. I've had this happen a
few times.

In the sense that a creative project dominates your dreams
and waking thoughts, it is a way of life. How you fit in the rest
of daily existence is part of the challenge, and, of course, the joy.

37

Silver Screen

I think of myself not as a screenwriter but as a novelist who, like many novelists, dabbles from time to time in film. Someone once explained to me that, as the author of one screenplay that actually came out as a movie, one novel that came out as a movie, and several screenplays that didn't get made but were paid for, I have had what constitutes an enviable career in film. "Any L.A. waiter or taxi driver waiting for someone to read his screenplay would envy you," a Los Angeles friend and agent assured me.

Of course I've been sorry that most of these efforts came to naught, but if I feel discouraged, I can think of many informative adventures screenwriting has brought me anyhow. How else could I have found myself on the catwalk of a Las Vegas casino, gazing through the mirrored ceiling to spy on the dealers and players; looking at Leonardo da Vincis in the velveted darkened room of a New York art dealer; talking to Luc Montagnier, the codiscoverer of the AIDS virus, and his rival, Robert Gallo; spending a week with polygamists? These things would be nothing to real journalists, say, but exciting for the more sedentary novelist. It hasn't escaped me, either, that these are the things people often want to hear about, not novel writing, which is after all a drab and solitary pursuit.

Screenwriting does get you around, and in my case has brought me into contact with some great directors, who are not like novelists or professors or any other category of human except maybe generals, or CEOs; and they are not like one another.

People in an audience always ask about them during question periods, and so because some whom I've met are getting elderly— two are dead now—the anecdotes that follow are not intended as serious film criticism so much as film history, about Mike Nich-ols, Francis Ford Coppola, Sydney Pollack, Stanley Kubrick, the German director Volker Schlöndorff, and, most recently, James Ivory, and not counting one lunch with Warren Beatty. Ivory made one of my novels, *Le Divorce*, into a film, where, though I didn't write the script, I did hang around the set quite a bit; for the others I wrote scripts, though I was sort of a jinx, it seemed, and except for *The Shining* they didn't turn out the way we'd hoped.

1

The project with Volker Schlöndorff was a film about the life of a Mormon martyr, John Singer, who was killed in a celebrated stand against the Utah state police in 1979 when he refused to hand over his second wife's children to Utah authorities after a custody battle. This was a story that resonated for Volker because John Singer was an immigrant from Germany, and, like Volker, had been shadowed by the wartime events of his boyhood. Writing the script required us to go to Utah, where we stayed in a pleasant hotel in Park City and went every day to interview John Singer's widow, Vickie Singer, who still lived in the place where Singer had been shot, with their children: the oldest boy, who was paralyzed from a logging accident; two daughters, who were both married to the same young man, Addam Swapp, with several little tow-headed tots between them; and some younger kids of Vickie's— six Singer kids in all, and the grandchildren. The place was a ramshackle compound of main house, small shabby cabins for the married daughters, and a little schoolhouse where the Singers had tried to homeschool their kids, though these efforts petered out; an impasse over the state-monitored tests precipitated the crisis that led to John Singer's death.

Like the family at Ruby Ridge, like fundamentalist families who come into the news every so often, the surviving Singers were violently antigovernment, bitter, and defiant. Vickie talked to us because she wanted her story known, and she wanted us to understand enough about Mormonism to see the rectitude of their fundamentalist views. Her enemies were other Mormons too—the Singers stood accused of apostasy (the title of our film) but had texts and writings to prove their theological case, which Vickie would read passionately to us. Some were the writings of John Singer, elevated in her mind to the infallibility of Joseph Smith himself.

These writings defended polygamy, homeschooling, civil disobedience, and unwavering faith. Vickie exemplified faith. Although she was or could have been a beautiful woman, she had suffered dental problems, and had to have all her teeth pulled out, and she refused to have false ones. Her beauty, except for toothlessness, made her even stranger than she would otherwise seem, her toothlessness an affront, a violation of what she was meant to be, and she seemed to relish the shock it gave others. The daughters were beautiful as well: Charlotte, a skinny sixteen-year-old blonde, expecting her first baby, and Heidi, the older, a blooming, sturdy redhead, with beautiful long braids down her back, and three kids in three years. Both were fierce defenders of their mother; Heidi had literally defended her father too, rushing at the Utah state police when she was twelve, armed with a small bow and arrows.

We would talk to Vickie all day, an exhausting but riveting process, then go to our hotel and spend the evenings writing our script. When it came to the ending, after the climax, the shooting of Singer, Volker and I disagreed. He saw mainly the sadness of the family, the fidelity of Vickie, the funeral, the triumph of violence and strong-arm tactics over the righteous believers. I saw the fanaticism of Vickie Singer, and wanted her to say, at John Singer's funeral in our script, "He is not dead. He will rise again. He will be avenged."

Events were to prove me right about Vickie's fanatic convictions. A few years after this, she and her oldest son, Tim, and the son-in-law, Addam, husband of the two daughters, bombed the Mormon church in a nearby town. This time too something went wrong. On January 16, 1988, two days before the ninth anniversary of the death of John Singer, Addam Swapp stuck a spear in the ground near the church, with the date of Singer's death—January 18, 1979—engraved on it, and nine feathers attached to the handle, broke into the Kamas LDS Stake Center, and filled the cultural hall with fifty pounds of dynamite and ammonium nitrate, which doubled the explosive force. The bomb was detonated at three in the morning and caused more than a million dollars' worth of damage. This act of terrorism was their way of notifying the mainstream Mormon Church and Utah that they had begun their revenge, which they called "atonement." Tracks in the snow led from the spear directly to the Singer farm.

When police contacted Addam Swapp and Vickie Singer and ordered them to surrender, they resisted. The officers who came to arrest them used the usual siege techniques—loud music, lights—and one of the policemen, a dog handler, was shot. Addam and Tim would say at their trial that they were trying to hit the dog. They were imprisoned, Addam in Arizona to spare him the vengeance of Utah correctional officers for his role in the killing of one of their colleagues. Tim was released in about 2006. Addam was paroled in 2013.

For our film, Volker liked to see Vickie as a crazy but touching example of wifely devotion, a tigress roused to defend her cubs. I saw a somewhat more sinister detail, maybe a female point of view. Before his death, John Singer had recently taken another wife, putting into practice the polygamy they all professed to believe in. This was his death warrant, I think, for Vickie, outwardly com‑ pliant, inwardly enraged, may have provoked him into the intrac‑ table furies that would bring him down. I think going toothless was a gesture of despair, but punishment of him too, disfiguring herself as an erotic object.

Our film was never made because in the end, despite her co‑ operation, Vickie refused to sign releases and permissions. We could have changed the names, or set the film somewhere else, but it would have lost some of the interest lent by reality, and Volker couldn't raise the money. A few years ago, I heard a rumor that some Australian director might revive the project, and it surprised me that things could stay alive so long, but I've never seen Volker again. During our Utah stay he was in the process of breaking up with his wife, the German director Margarethe von Trotta, and he had a new girlfriend in Germany, to whom he would talk for expensive, agonizing hours on the phone when we were done working and it became morning in Germany; and Utah may have finished him for the United States, because he

left soon after. Who knows if he's ever come back? I have heard
that he remarried, became a father, and for a while ran the German film industry center, and makes films there that rarely get
to America. Margarethe goes on making films, for instance the
recent interesting history of Hannah Arendt and her take on the
banality of evil.

For some time I would send Heidi Singer Swapp a little check,
thinking of the poor young woman, no money, all those babies—
she and Charlotte had six between them before Addam was taken
away—and she would write polite thank-you letters, wistful letters wondering what Paris was like; but then I sent her some tourist books about France and never thereafter heard from her, as if
something about them had shocked her, appalled her, unlike hers
a world so garlanded with ostentatious symbols of sin.

2

And now I'm in a Hawker Siddeley executive jet belonging to
MGM, jetting to Las Vegas, where Mike Nichols and I will
spend a few days as guests of the MGM Grand Hotel. Nichols
and the Hawker were obliged to swoop down to get me at the
airport in Bloomington, Illinois, the airport nearest Chenoa, Illinois, where my mother and I were visiting my aunt Henrietta.

She and Mother drove me to the airport. "Shouldn't you
check in?" they kept saying, and I kept explaining that the plane
wouldn't leave without me, yet how astonished we all were as the
elegant little plane really alit, Nichols got out, gravely greeting
the aunts and my mother, and we took off. He had been asked
by MGM to remake one of their classic films, *Grand Hotel*. The
original Grand Hotel of Vicki Baum's novel and the Garbo film

was in Berlin, but this one was to be set in the studio-owned Grand Hotel in Las Vegas. On this field trip we'd learn details of the hotel/casino structure, and soak up the Nevada ambiance.

"But we won't gamble," Nichols said. I agreed, am not drawn to gambling, had spent too many hours in the car in Reno while my parents went in to the craps table, or it seemed hours, though they denied that this was possible, or, if it happened, could have been only once, for a few minutes. Anyway, who would want to gamble and be just like the hundreds of unattractive, seedy, old-looking people who stood around pulling slot machines, carrying wax paper cups of quarters? Droves of them getting off buses from L.A. or from Reno, wearing polyester. It was clear to us that the MGM hotel was not a classy place; neither was Las Vegas in general, and if there had been days of glamour and high rollers, these days were gone. Now they are back, I'm told, brought by imitation Venetian canals, an Eiffel Tower, real three-star French restaurants, and serious art; but at the time of our visit, this up-grade hadn't happened. The closest thing to art I saw in Las Ve-gas was Siegfried and Roy's copy of the Sistine Chapel ceiling.

Nichols and I liked crawling around on the catwalks and into the secret observation places where all the mirrors are one-way. Through the mirrored ceilings, the hotel management watches the dealers, watches for counters, watches for drunks and known hookers. They are looking to keep the place "clean," or appar-ently clean, minimize cheating by their own dealers, eradicate skimming, and reduce the discord that can erupt if the tables aren't well run.

There is about one day of interest in all this, however, and then the boredom sets in, excruciating by the third or fourth day. There are no clocks, as is well known, and the lights are always on, as in a torture cell. I hid out more and more in my room, which was decorated in purple satin and had an oval bath-tub in the middle of it. I forget who was playing in the floor show. Maybe we didn't go in to see it. Nichols made me laugh in the elaborately pretentious French restaurant dining room by speaking French, finally forcing the waiter to say, "What are you saying? I don't understand you."

"What? Oh, sorry, isn't this a French restaurant? I was just trying to fit in."

Boredom leads to gambling, which must be the idea behind causing time to cease. Inevitably we drifted to the tables, and decided to play chemin de fer, which Mike had heard had slightly better odds than other games. I forget how you play it, but it is very, very simple, something like war, or spit, suited to merry but nonintellectual aristocrats at Monte Carlo and the like, and in Las Vegas attracted the smartest set, who were, even so, disap-pointingly not fashionable, not evening-gowned or bejeweled—nothing like John Barrymore's fellow gamblers in the earlier film.

We had each brought two hundred dollars and resolved to stop when it was gone. Mine was soon gone, and that was okay, but Nichols's blood was up, just as he'd feared, and he was obliged to ask the cashier for more money. He had his credit cards, his checkbook; he was of course marvelously solvent. Nonetheless the rules are the rules, and never mind that we were guests of the hotel, with all his millions, he could not get more cash. There was no one in authority who could authorize high rolling, no sleek-haired mobsters in wide-shouldered suits coming out from the back room to take special care of a special customer, no mecha-nism for finding out who anyone was. The relentless democracy and low expectations of a Las Vegas casino destroyed any belief we might have had in the existence of an aristocracy of gamblers, no genre elegance of the kind seen in movies, only tawdriness, depressing in the lowness of its sights and the modesty of its table limits.

Obviously the movie could not be realistic on this point; it would have by definition to be a lie, or it had to tell the truth in such a way that MGM wouldn't recognize it, because they wanted to stress the glamour of their hotel. The truth would have to slip by, tongue-in-cheek. That was what we tried for in the script, in which Nichols saw someone like Dolly Parton in the Garbo role, and Warren Beatty as the Baron—John Barrymore in the old film. In our update, he'd be the president of Ford or GM, in Las Vegas for an automobile convention.

We went back to New York and blocked out a schedule for working on the script that involved my flying in from Paris, where I was living—this must have been 1986 or so—for week-long sessions over the next few months. I stayed in the Carlyle Hotel, where he lived, and we set about blocking out the details of the film.

Nichols is a delightful, smart, and funny man, and if he has a difficult side, it didn't manifest itself during our work together.

At the time, he was interested in adding to his art collection, and wanted to go look at a number of paintings. He already had a memorable Balthus, and some other things, and a reputation as a serious collector, which brought out an especially unctuous solicitousness from art dealers. An art dealer would call; we would fling down our papers, and I would go with him to very grand art galleries, where we would sit in darkened rooms in front of easels draped in black velvet. Reverently, the dealers would bring out a Van Gogh, a Picasso, even a bust presumed to

be by Michelangelo. Some were unbelievably ugly—it made
you aware that if these things were real, then even Van Gogh
had bad days. It's clear anyhow that art dealers will sell any old
scrap that falls from a master's hand, and that there are pitfalls
for the unwary in the great world of art collecting. In any case,
Nichols, a man of taste, declined these wares in the politest way
imaginable.

But before our film project collapsed of its own defects—or
maybe it would have succeeded, and it certainly would have been
fun—we were spared rejection by the fire that destroyed the MGM
Grand Hotel, one of the first and biggest high-rise fires that ex-
posed the dangers of plastic and Styrofoam, and it would take years
to rebuild. The film lost its point for MGM, and eventually Nichols
went on to other things, and so did I. He must be amused about the
recent scandal in Northern Ireland, where the prime minister's
wife, Mrs. Robinson, confessed to an affair with a nineteen-year-old,
life imitating the art of his famous movie *The Graduate*.

3

In 1992, Francis Ford Coppola had a brilliant idea for making an
AIDS movie about the worsening and still poorly understood
epidemic. What he had in mind was not a sad movie about the
victims but a movie about the scientists searching for the cure
for an elusive and baffling and uniformly fatal disease. The film
would be called, in fact, *CURE*, and the project involved a double brief—to write the script and, if possible, in real life (for
Francis dreams big), discover or synthesize some bit of information that had eluded the scientists, some clue or connection that
only art could make that would, in fact, help lead to a cure.
CURE.

Because I had some film and some medical background (as a doctor's wife), I was hired to write the script, and Jessica Abbe, a young filmmaker and friend, was to help me with the research, which would begin with interviews of leading scientists. We talked to Anthony Fauci, an immunologist and sort of czar appointed in 1984 to be in charge of NIAID (the National Institute of Allergy and Infectious Diseases), guiding the AIDS research effort; the vivid Robert Gallo; Jerome Groopman, at that time overseeing the treatment of many high-profile victims; and many other American scientists. And in France, to Luc Montagnier and Françoise Barré-Sinoussi, who recently shared the Nobel Prize for discovering the virus; Jacques Liebovitz; Daniel Zagury (known then for injecting himself with an experimental AIDS vaccine he was developing in Zaire); Jonas Salk; and many others. I also talked to Randy Shilts, Larry Kramer, and other leading activists, and various organizers, including Elizabeth Taylor, who led, and whose foundation still leads, an important fund-raising effort.

At one point, Francis, Jessie, and I went to Amsterdam for a week for the international AIDS conference (staying in the best hotel), which is where we had coffee with Taylor (who, from where I was sitting, at her elbow, looked fantastic, in her sixties, though maybe more elaborately coiffed and made up for a morning visit than ordinary people would be). I became distracted with the wish to know what if anything she'd had done to her famous, perfect face, and who'd done it, but never could see any traces—no telltale scars behind the ears, for instance. Her then husband, Larry Fortensky, was there too—and pretty cute with his long blond hair. He was the one she'd met at the Betty

Ford Center—a former construction worker. Eventually they divorced, but then he was still an apparently cheerful presence in
her life.

Jessie and I went to meetings, met scientists, took notes, and
developed ideas for a three-part script that would follow virologists, biologists, and epidemiologists, working at the NIH, in Africa, and in medical practices and labs. At this period, much
wasn't clear about the disease, including whether it was actually
caused by HIV, the virus discovered by Montagnier and/or Gallo.
The origin is still an issue debated in some parts of Africa.

We saw little of Francis, though he would meet us for the most
amusing events; for instance, he and I had dinner with Jonas Salk
one night. Physically, Salk reminded me quite a bit of S. J. Perel-
man, whom I'd interviewed once in connection with a biography I
was writing of Dashiell Hammett: small, slender, white-haired, sar-
donic men. With Salk, we talked, naturally, about vaccines. Francis also went to some of the scientific meetings, where he caused a
gratifying stir; but he stayed in his room a lot too.

It was becoming generally clear to us that scientists in, say,
the field of vaccine development were not very interested in what
the cell biologists were doing, nor were other basic scientists—
hematologists, virologists, and clinicians—paying much attention to the rival disciplines. The specialties didn't overlap, the
labs were often widely separated, and they competed with one
another for research funds. These in turn were doled out by Anthony Fauci, who is still in charge at NIAID, a good administra-
tor and good scientist but not a unifier in this situation. To us
nonscientists, it seemed like scientific chaos.

"These people need a director," Francis said. Even Jessie and

I began to share his dream of having some flash of insight not
available to mere scientists, some artistic intuition that could
lead to a solution to the problem that had eluded them, some
idea that would cause the scientific research to coalesce. Pursu-
ing this, when we got back from Amsterdam, Francis organized
an AIDS weekend conference to be held at his beautiful Victorian house and grounds in Napa, and we were all surprised and
pleased at how many of the great names in science agreed to attend, from France, from Baltimore, from Washington, and from
the various labs around America that were involved in the research.

He made the great scientists play the party games that actors
are made to play—like miming their morning rituals. Françoise
Barré-Sinoussi mimed putting her contact lenses in first thing,
then brushing her teeth. (I noticed in her Nobel Prize photos that
she wears her glasses now.) The scientists passed oranges from
chin to chin, smiling into one another's eyes, they talked to people
in other specialties, and more than one agreed it had been helpful,
even startlingly so. "I never knew what those guys at Duke were
doing," and so on. Virologists didn't usually read immunology
journals, but now there were panel discussions and informal
meals—it was all a great success. Jessie and I had the secret opinion that Francis liked the role of AIDS director more than he
liked script work, for absent his input we weren't really getting
very far with our story, though we had begun to have some ideas
of the direction science itself ought to be taking. And it was plain
that the AIDS research effort had need of someone like Francis to
coordinate more effectively than was being done by the NIH.

I blocked out a structure for the film, and some tentative directions we could pursue. Francis frowned over the first page,

which involved two models looking mournfully down at the fresh grave of their late boss, a fashion designer dead from AIDS. "Let me show you how it should be done." He took away my page and came back in an hour with a brilliant rendition of the scene—it made me know I'd never be a serious screenwriter, because though I can do the structure, and the dialogue, I'll never get the knack of making the stage directions vivid, in passages I would once have thought of as being overwritten: "INTERIOR. DAY. A brilliant ray of May sun streams through the tall window of a somber chamber heavily draped in funereal folds of green velvet. A sorrowing woman in black Saint Laurent bows her suavely coiffed blond head. . . ." Detailed so that the studio exec (as opposed to the eventual viewer) can envision the scene before it gets to the screen. Kubrick had also pleaded for my stage directions to be a little more frilly for those readers. I understand intellectually the need for this, but when it comes to it, something in me can't do it very well—the absence of a poetic bone or the ghost of Hemingway shaking his head.

Our story concerned three main scientists in three interwoven stories, representing virology, bacteriology, cell biology, gene therapy, and so on, on three fronts of the AIDS epidemic, in California, Africa, and the National Institutes of Health in Washington. Strange to say, the solution we came up with for the cure was not far from the triple therapy that real scientists eventually found, drawing from the disciplines we tried to write about.

When I had managed, with input from Jessie, to carve out a rough first draft, almost before we had talked about the script with him, Francis organized to have it read out loud. Actors were found by a Zoetrope casting director, a place in North Beach was reserved, a small audience convened. Already daunted by this seriousness, I was flattened by horror when I heard the first creaky lines, all the things that didn't work. I had had the same reaction when I heard the first words of *The Shining*—I would have rewritten every speech. Francis waxed enthusiastic: Let's shoot it! Pirated copies of the script were on the street the next day. What a horrible experience.

It would turn out, though, that Francis was through with filmmaking for a while, I hope not driven out because of *CURE*. A few weeks after this, he shut down things around Zoetrope and turned to his wine empire, and for years he made no movies—only later returning to make two more personal films, *Youth Without Youth* and *Tetro*.

4

When my novel *Le Divorce* came out in 1997, it was bought by Ballpark Films, then a division of PolyGram, which in turn was owned by Seagram's or something—one of those film world boxes within boxes. The producer, Michael Schiffer, was a passionate Francophile, and had spent time in France, traveled around, fallen in love, and had always wanted to make a French film. I wrote a script, and he began to look around for a director. I suggested Merchant Ivory, as I was among the fans of their elegant and literary films. This was when I was made aware of a sort of general prejudice in the minds of many Hollywood movie people about independent films, which, however, have gained a lot in respectability since then. Merchant Ivory had just brought out *A Soldier's Daughter Never Cries*—a wonderful movie shot in Paris, based on a book by Kaylie Jones, the daughter of the novelist James Jones, and I suggested that Schiffer and the agents at Creative Artists Agency go see this terrific film. No way. It wouldn't occur to a Hollywood regular to go see a Merchant Ivory film, so absolute was their mistrust of independent productions, Merchant Ivory's fabled low budgets, and so on, never mind their Oscar nominations and the continued popularity of their films. Ballpark and CAA continued to look elsewhere, without success.

Meantime, coincidentally, I had lunch with Jim Ivory in Paris; he had already had his eye on my novel—a matter of his buying out the present owners when they despaired of it, which is what happened. I greatly enjoyed the chance to watch *Le Divorce* being filmed—I had seen too little of the shooting of *The Shining;* and now here was a film being shot in my neighborhood in Paris and just across town. I could pop in, watch for a while, leave, come back—I did try not to get in the way but would hover mouselike on the sidelines. They weren't filming my own script, which, according to Writers Guild rules, they would have had to buy from Ballpark (which had already paid me), so Ivory wrote another, with his frequent collaboratrice, the late Ruth Prawer Jhabvala.

I thought it was very good, except for a difference we had about the ending. The story is about a young California woman's fling in Paris. In Jhabvala's version, Isabel, the heroine, becomes pregnant, the older lover doesn't stand by her, suggests an abortion, she bravely decides to keep the baby—rather as in the ending of *Howards End,* Merchant Ivory's film of E. M. Forster's novel. I wasn't sure of the reason for Jhabvala's alterations. Perhaps the filmmakers wanted to introduce moral accountability, some sense that women must pay for sexual transgressions; it happens to be the very archetype I seriously wished to flout by allowing Isabel to learn other lessons, but not that one, which I don't believe.

When I went to the first showing, not knowing about the

changed ending, I was dumbfounded, and so was Fox Search-
light, which was putting up the money. Isabel's waters breaking
in the Place Vendôme? Studio execs cried out in protest, above
all Michael Schiffer, the original purchaser of the book and its
loyal supporter. A new, less dramatic ending was shot, closer to
the original, in which the couple breaks up, and the inveterate
seducer and a resigned and wiser Isabel go their ways. In the
meantime, I had thought up a way the Jhabvala idea could have
made an amusing ending for the film—because the officious
French family would certainly have adored the baby, and I could
imagine Madame de Persand, Leslie Caron's character, knitting
little socks, with Isabel condemned to Sunday lunches with the
French family for the rest of her days.

It was inspiring to watch James Ivory work. On the surface gen-
tle and nondirective, he controlled every element, and of the directors I'd worked with, he displayed an overall hands-on attention to
detail and refined literary sensibility that most resembled
Kubrick's, even though their budgets differed wildly. The smaller
scale of the *Le Divorce* shoot was easier for me to grasp; the locations were here and there around Paris, in places like the Dior bou-
tique and the Café de Flore. Some scenes had to be shot at night in
places that were too busy to allow filming in the daytime. Once
good locations were found, Ivory did a minimum of tinkering with
the decor, but I do remember plants being brought in, and blue
cloth pinned over the khaki-colored walls of a beautiful seventeenth-
century *hôtel particulier* belonging to the Schlumbergers—in which
the novelist Mrs. Pace lives, Glenn Close's role in the film. The
producer, Ismail Merchant, was known for his ability to charm
people into lending their houses for Merchant Ivory films. Some of
the props—in particular a fake Georges de La Tour painting of

St. Ursula—had been created by one of those experts you see copying paintings in the Louvre. The result was so beautiful and convincing that Ivory kept it. I had hoped to buy it from the production myself. One of the characters gives a poetry reading in the movie, from, ostensibly, her own poems. I do have the copy she read from, printed up like a real book with a new jacket; and also an auction catalog, beautifully convincing, with the La Tour on the cover. I treasure these film souvenirs, and, most notably, Mrs. Pace's coffee table, which, when I admired it, Ismail Merchant gave me.

I am sorry I never had a chance to watch Ismail Merchant at work on the strangely memorable and very expressive and original films on Indian subjects that he directed without James Ivory: among them, *Cotton Mary*, *The Mystic Masseur*, and my favorite, *The Proprietor*, with its haunting village scenes. The death of this charming and energetic man was a terrible loss for film. After Merchant's death, James Ivory made a wonderful film set in Uruguay, *The City of Your Final Destination*, from a novel by Peter Cameron, with all of the Merchant Ivory signature elements of rich surface and elegiac themes of promise and loss.

5

Over the years, other screenwriters have told about their work with Stanley Kubrick, and since his death their accounts seem of particular interest, both as a way of explicating his earlier work, which has remained the subject of critical discussion, and particularly as a way of illuminating his last work, *Eyes Wide Shut*, about which there is still no unified critical opinion except, perhaps, an impression, among American critics at least, that it doesn't quite work, and among French ones that it does. No one entirely agrees about its "meaning," which from reading *Rhapsody: A Dream Novel* I take as an allegory of male sexual psychology and the logic of dreams, under the influence of his friend Freud.

My own work with Kubrick in 1979 came about as a result of his reading my novel *The Shadow Knows*, a psychological novel with certain connections to the detective story, in my mind dealing with racial issues and urban violence, or, in the minds of some readers, about the deteriorating state of mind of a young woman under stress who is perhaps, or perhaps not, being stalked. Kubrick had been browsing in the horror genre because he wanted, he said, to make the scariest movie he could. He typically rose to genre challenges, and had already made a great science fiction movie, a historical film, a dystopian one, and was thinking about a war movie, partly, perhaps, challenged by rumors of Francis Ford Coppola's *Apocalypse Now*, then under way, to be released in 1979, a little before *The Shining*.

He didn't want to make a movie that depended unduly on ghosts and the supernatural for horrific effect. Though he didn't rule out the supernatural, it was to be a film in which the horror generated from human psychology. This was the case with my novel, and also with Stephen King's novel *The Shining*. There are some apparitions in the latter that can be taken for projections of the disturbed mind of the hero, Jack Torrance, or else as supernatural.

For whatever reason, in part certainly because my novel was a first-person narrative, therefore harder to film, Kubrick chose to use *The Shining* instead of *The Shadow Knows;* however, he chose me to write the script. One reason was that in connection with my university teaching, I had some acquaintance with the classic texts of gothic literature—*The Mysteries of Udolpho* and *The*

Monk, for example. In fact these would hardly come into it, but at least I could recommend some books for him to read. Literary himself, Kubrick believed in having an academic foundation in the subjects of his films, if only in his collaborators.

Parenthetically, *The Shadow Knows* has tempted several directors and producers. Faye Dunaway had it at one time; at another I was actually writing a script for Sydney Pollack—that nice man, now gone. We were in the middle of a script for *The Shadow Knows* when he was offered a chance to step in as the director of *Tootsie*, which someone had abandoned in midproduction, a decision I'm sure he never regretted. A good director and a good actor, as we saw in his cameo in *Eyes Wide Shut*.

Kubrick wanted to know what the King novel was about, in the deepest psychological sense; he wanted to talk about that, and read theoretical works that might shed light on it, particularly works of psychology and particularly Freud. Perhaps he also thought I would be freer (less respectful) and more flexible than the author himself in tampering with the text of *The Shining*— almost certainly the case. He sweetly soothed any disappointment I might have felt that he didn't choose my novel for his film by saying it was easier to make a film of a less literary work, or a major author's lesser work, for example Thackeray's *Barry Lyndon* instead of *Vanity Fair*.

He also believed in adapting books that already existed rather than working from original scripts. There were several reasons for this, mostly that you could gauge the effect, examine the structure, and think about the subject of a book more easily than in a script, and novelists, he thought, were apt to be better writers than screenwriters are—an idea that many would debate, no doubt. But for whatever reasons in his personal experience, he didn't have much respect for screenwriters per se, and tended to work with novelists—Terry Southern, Michael Herr, Arthur C. Clarke, Vladimir Nabokov, and so on.

From his point of view, it didn't matter and was even an advantage that I had had no screenwriting experience, and from my point of view, it was an excellent chance to learn something about this elusive craft. My arrangement with him was similar to that of other writers he worked with, before and after. "Be sure you don't live out there [near the Kubricks]; stay in London or your life won't be your own." This was the advice of Terry Southern (author of the *Dr. Strangelove* and *Lolita* scripts). I followed Terry's advice, rented a place in London, and was conveyed to Kubrick's house every day in an orange Mercedes, a trip of an hour or so. I enjoyed the Kubrick ménage. His wife, Christiane, was a serious painter and a good cook; you sat around the big, light kitchen of a house almost as big as the Overlook, our film hotel, and there were dogs and cats and the two Kubrick daughters, and people working on the art direction or the sets coming in and out. Kubrick was a motherly parent to all—dogs, cats, kids—and worried about minute details of their well-being. I especially remember when poor Teddy, his golden retriever, got lymphoma— his frantic calls to my doctor husband in California; consultations about vets testified to his tender heart toward, perhaps, everybody but actors. He said he didn't like actors, and loved every aspect of filmmaking except shooting.

Kubrick and I would work in the morning, face-to-face across a table in a big workroom. In the afternoon he turned to the other ongoing matters of the set, casting (which was mostly done), costume, the music, and so on, and I would often participate in these matters too, invited to comment as part of the process. So were members of his family, who came in and out, with views of their own. "Oh, Daddy, no one dresses like that." I remember objecting to one detail of the set—the way the tile in a bathroom went all the way up to the ceiling, "like a gas chamber. Bathroom tiles mostly stop at the height of the shower door." Kubrick had the tiles torn out. He would try out different tapes and records on the family, and everyone commented on the music. I believe this evolving and organic way of attending to all the aspects of a film at the same time is an improvement on the more common practice, by many directors, of seeing how the script will come out before beginning to plan the production; the commitment built into the process in the former case enriches it.

But perhaps it works best when the whole family is, like the Kubricks, interested in the ongoing process. Still, it was certainly Kubrick himself who presented the options and initiated discussion of the various elements of music, casting, decor, and the like. He was an artist, with the inner life of one, dreaming about his work, given to inspirations that would come on suddenly—as novelists are.

I would hang around till evening, we'd have dinner and watch movies. We'd watch other horror movies, old Jack Nicholson films (was he better playing a depressed or manic character?), classics, and things that were playing in the West End at the moment. Eventually, the chauffeur would take me back to London; the script was written in eleven weeks altogether. Once in a while the Kubricks would come back to London with me to have dinner with literary friends of mine, people Stanley had heard of and wanted to meet, the book world being somehow shut off from the film world in England at that time. He was a great admirer of Harold Pinter, and when they met, Stanley became shy and affable.

Much of our work time was spent talking about and planning the sequence of scenes; the words themselves, when we arrived at them, were relatively simple; it is not a very "talky" script, and the final version even less so than my script, which had much more for Wendy Torrance to say than she ultimately says. I had gotten interested in Wendy and gave her some sympathetic lines, more in the spirit of King's book. Though I did not watch the filming, Shelley Duvall told me later that she and Kubrick were often at odds, and that he cut a lot of her lines. He told me, as I remember, that she couldn't say them right. The result was not the "round" Wendy, as I had hoped to characterize her (and as King does characterize her), but a snivelly character reduced to tears and whimpers.

Ultimately there were a number of cuts from the script, or from the film itself, above all in its shorter European version. One I found especially unfortunate when I finally saw the film, at a screening Kubrick arranged in London a few weeks after it had actually come out. For me, an important scene in Stephen King's novel is where Jack, a blocked writer, discovers a scrapbook of clippings in the boiler room of the hotel, and finds in it plots and details he needs to get going on his writing. In King's book, this is the Faustian bargain, or poison gift of fairy tales, which, when he accepts it, entangles the hero in consequences he will regret. In accepting material to help him earn literary glory, he barters his soul, and becomes the creature of the hotel. This motivation scene existed in the script and I understand the scene was shot, but it was taken out of the final cut for reasons of time. It would be interesting to see it restored, to know what it would add. Without the scene, which explains Jack's transition from depressed and blocked writer to one suddenly filled with demonic energy, writing at great speed and piling high the pages of manuscript, his change seems abrupt and unmotivated.

For Stephen King, I gather from his miniseries remake of *The Shining*, the character flaws of the father were of less interest than the supernatural powers of foresight of Danny, the little boy; and the hotel was the true villain, an evil force locked in combat with the good child. For Kubrick, it was the character of the father that interested, and the powers of the boy were mainly intuitive, a child's heightened sensitivity to the demons rising in the adults who have power over him. To what extent supernatural forces exist, and to what extent these are psychological projections, was something we discussed at length, finally deciding that the ghosts and magical apparitions at the Overlook Hotel were both, that the supernatural is somehow generated by human psychology, but, once generated, really exists and has power. Can Lloyd, the ghostly caretaker/bartender, open a door, for instance, to let Jack out of the freezer? The answer had to be yes.

Kubrick was concerned that the movie be scary, but what makes something scary? We sought the answer in the works of Freud, especially in his essay on the uncanny, and in other psychological theories for why things frighten us, and about what things are frightening, for instance the sudden animation of an inanimate figure. Dark is scary. Eyes can be scary. Kubrick would avail himself of these and other traditional ingredients of horror, for instance the moldering corpse of the woman in the bathtub, which was also in Stephen King's book. But it was typical of him to want an explanation for the nature of horror, wanting to understand the underlying psychological mechanism. Thus he wanted a "rational" explanation for the haunting of the hotel, and was drawn to the idea that the place rested on the site of Indian massacres or that

building it had desecrated some Native American tombs, with all
the ghosts and hauntings summoned thereby. Clearly, he had no
objection to the idea of something being haunted, that is, of the
supernatural per se; it was just that there had to be a reason for it.
He didn't mind living with the paradox of something being both
true and impossible at the same time.

Geoffrey Cocks, in his essay on some of the symbols in *The
Shining*, has suggested Kubrick's preoccupation with the Holocaust, and his interest in the extermination of Indian peoples,
might reinforce this idea. Certainly a Holocaust connection was
never mentioned to me or discussed as part of his conscious in-
tention, but of course the whole notion that unconscious motifs
creep into Kubrick's films the way they would into any novelist's
novels, without the conscious collusion of the artist, is possible.
In the finished film, the idea of tainted ground and Indian ghosts
malevolently hovering over the hotel does not really achieve vi-
sual or other expression, or only subliminally—one critic points
out the Calumet baking powder tin in Wendy's kitchen—but it
served to generate some of the creativity of the filmmaker, and
some of the decor.

It has been alleged of Kubrick—one could almost say he has
been *accused* of intellectualism, by which is usually meant being
too smart, one of the strangest objections to art, and one that is
taken too easily and without examining the ways in which intellectualism is in fact a necessary approach to art, even if not its
wellspring. To me it seemed that Kubrick's rational and analytic
approach to the complex matters of filmmaking was part of the
essence of his genius. Film is not a medium where one should
plunge in with high hopes and a vague idea. The novelist can, to
a certain extent, wing it into a new work, though even with the

novel, a certain amount of preplanning is indispensable, and the more that can be known in advance of writing, the greater the room for inspiration.

We began by each deconstructing King's novel separately, reducing it to essential scenes, then compared our lists of scenes, and winnowed them down to a hundred or so. I tore bits of exposition and dialogue out of a paperback copy and put them in little envelopes on which were written "#1 the Arrival," and so on. I still use the scissors I used to cut the pages—Kubrick being most considerate of his writers and insistent that they have the equipment most comfortable for them: which typewriter would you like? (An Adler electric, just as Kubrick used and Jack uses in the film.) Scissors? Size and color of paper? He had his own habits when it came to colors of paper—for some reason the pages I still have are pink or blue. These colors represented the drafts at various stages. Left to myself, I would never use pink or blue paper to write on (only yellow), but it seems I was docile in the case of this system of color coding.

Next came the process of deciding on a definitive structure, that is, which scenes, which additional scenes, and in which order. We used an eight-act structure divided roughly into timed sequences, sketched out by Kubrick into First Day; Day of the Psychiatrist; Arrival; Before the Snow (things are going well); Snow (lull); Big Day (argument, radio dead, finds scrapbook, key to room 217, Lloyd, Jack to room 217); Night Scene (with snowcat distributor cap); last, Elevator (calls to Halloran, last twenty-four hours of terror). He saw the first four sections as lasting forty-six minutes and the rest seventy-six—which of course the film greatly exceeded.

This was a world in which supernatural things would happen.

The ghosts of the hotel had appropriated Jack's soul, and would show him shades and past events. But certain rules applied. No artist would be an artist if he did not review and modify his principles, and one of Kubrick's most firm ones was that there should be no violations of the basic verisimilitude. He would permit no unbelievable things of the kind that are seen in too many films; for example, where the character who decides to jump into a car and escape finds the keys already in it. The world of film can be a fantasy world, but within its terms it must conform to what we know of the real world. Critics initially complained about the "unbelievable" things in Kubrik's last film, *Eyes Wide Shut,* a film about the male psyche: How does the Tom Cruise character have so much money in his wallet? Why are none of the street names correct? In a sense the answer is self-evident, and certainly the title of Arthur Schnitzler's *Rhapsody: A Dream Novel* specifies the dream nature of the hero's experience. In a dream you have the money. A texture of unconscious fears and wishes unfolds—a lover waltzes away with your wife, a patient's pretty daughter confesses her love for you, a prostitute both beckons and represents death, the erotic fantasies of men about little girls are made frighteningly specific. It is all about the buried fear, desire, and omnipresence of sex, preoccupations with death, the connection of death and eros, and above all the anxiety generated in men by female sexuality—Freudian subjects, also Schnitzler's subjects. It seems that Kubrick took some care to situate it not in the real but in some dream version of the world, just as in Schnitzler's story.

I think this would have been clearer and more effective set in the period of Schnitzler's writing, 1926, when the idea that women had sexual desires was startling, even unacceptable. Set in modern times, Tom Cruise's dismay at his wife's sexy dream merely seems peculiar or willfully egotistical and takes away our sympathy and credulity. The same with the orgy that people found so banal. The point, surely, is that it is an archetypal orgy, decorated with clichés and images from the collective unconscious—cats, masks, and so on.

Kubrick had the reputation, even in the 1980s, of being savage, difficult, reclusive. This is the persona that had so animated Frederic Raphael's belligerent apprehensions before they even met, as he recounts in his book *Eyes Wide Open*, about their experiences together in writing *Eyes Wide Shut*. I would have said that my own harmonious work with him had some other explanation—the fact that I was a woman, perhaps—except that Michael Herr's experience for *Full Metal Jacket* was pretty much like mine. We both thought Kubrick was terrific—nice, funny, wonderfully smart, and inspiring—an authentic auteur, his works the considered products of a major artistic sensibility.

Now I wish I had taken notes of more of the details of my life at the Kubricks', and at other times in my life, for that matter. Looking back, I seem to have noticed too little about the moment I was in, and had not much eye for the eventual historical interest of things either, and what I remember is so often a trivial detail, of little interest to posterity—the look of Christiane's flower beds, or the chauffeur's ramblings about Mussolini.

I have no news of Volker Schlöndorff, and Kubrick is dead. It's hard not to wax philosophical on the futility of human effort, but I've often thought about one thing certain: if you want to be a successful screenwriter, you have to have a lot of hopeful energy and optimism, a lot of belief that your film is really going to come about. I think I have always had too fatalistic a view: it will happen or it won't. Probably you have to work and strategize. On the other hand, as the agent said, my movie career has been by most standards enviable. Maybe, but I'll always wonder if some deficit of talent or lapse of attention of my own had somehow set that Grand Hotel fire, or chilled the ardor of the German producers.

I may have been a jinx.

38

Uncle Bill

When my children were small, I had to put my uncle Bill in the madhouse. It took me a long time to come to terms with Uncle Bill's story and my role in it. It is interesting the retrospective way we learn, as events are revealed or ferreted out, or as a little mention is let drop.

Uncle Bill Dobie, a lean Scotsman, was married to my father's sister Ruth. It was from Uncle Bill and Aunt Ruth I learned that life could go wrong. It didn't seem possible that anything could derail the perfect life of this handsome, loving, and cheerful pair. He was a wildly devoted husband, slightly younger than my adorable aunt Ruth, and she was equally mad about him. There was a shadow, though.

They were so fond of me, I eventually understood, because they had lost their own year-old baby to pneumonia, and what with my aunt's age and problem pregnancy, they hadn't tried again for another child, but focused all their parental love on their little niece. Their love took many forms, sometimes exigent ("Hold your back up!"), but included a sumptuous wardrobe of little dresses—because my uncle was a buyer in a department store; dolls; a long visit to Sioux City, Iowa, each summer; and eventually visits to Sioux Falls, South Dakota, where they moved with Uncle Bill's promotion in the course of his rising career. We were given to understand this was a stressful career because retailing was capricious, you never knew if you would guess right what women would buy and in what quantities.

I wonder what Sioux Falls looks like now. In those days it had fine big turn-of-the-century houses with dumbwaiters and vast lawns. My friends Lou and Dede lived in such a house; we scampered after fireflies on the lawn. Now, I've read, it is hard even to get to South Dakota—the train, the plane, even the Greyhound, seldom go there. But in those days, my parents would confide me, with a five-dollar bill, to the care of the porter in charge of the train car, and he would deliver me safely to my waiting aunt and uncle. I believe I made my first train journey like this when I was four. I mention this to contrast the conditions of then and now, when my parents would be imprisoned for child neglect.

As I was growing up, uncles and golfers and card playing were synonymous in my mind. I don't remember any adult conversations from my childhood that didn't concern handicaps or the conditions of the greens, unless it was family gossip or Roosevelt. Uncle Bill was the best golfer among my uncles. To make up for his nervous temperament, Uncle Bill had been given this gift in life, to be a superior golfer, and from that, and his wit and my aunt's gaiety, arose their popularity. My uncle was president of the country club, my aunt was in all the women's organizations (including one, PEO, so secret she couldn't tell me what PEO stood for—now I've Googled it: Philanthropic Educational Organization). They were Masons, Kiwanis, Elks. They went to lots of parties. It was the days of scotch and sodas and Cadillacs. My aunt would have liked a Cadillac, but they only had a DeSoto. "Someday, baby doll," said my uncle with a wink.

It was with Aunt Ruth and Uncle Bill that I had many of my first important experiences—learned to swim, for example, and learned to eat Roquefort cheese. I can't explain the impulse that led them to smear some on a cracker and give it to me when I was four, a picky eater who resisted even ice cream and cookies. I think it was connected to the fact that they had company.

I'd learned the value of performance. I'd been mildly traumatized by an incident in preschool, when the role of bandleader, almost mine, had been taken instead by a more vivid, animated child. It was Marjorie Young who got to wield the stick and wear the cape, while I was relegated to playing the triangle. Now I ate the cheese, smiled at the audience, thriving on their amazement, their joy, praise of my worldliness and adaptability, the care that had been taken with my upbringing to produce such a flexible, adventurous tot.

I also found that I was eating something delicious, different from our usual fare of pot roast and potatoes. It was almost the first food I liked, and this in turn suggested vistas of possibility, food horizons beyond Moline and Sioux Falls, South Dakota—it was probably in fact a local cheese called Nauvoo Blue, but France was mentioned. All summer long I would hear myself praised: only four, just loves Roquefort cheese . . . France.

Aunt Ruth and Uncle Bill delighted in what they imagined was my precociousness—they knew very few children—which they gleefully fostered with books and big words. They wanted me to grow up to be beautiful and richly married; it was their principal hope. And, I later learned, they wanted me not to kill myself.

Another nephew, Jim, the son of one of my father's brothers, Uncle Guy, had killed himself while living with them, another of their tragedies; one day when they were out, he put the gas on and no one knew why. His sister Dorothy had done it earlier, a young married woman—and no one knew why she did it either. Something in the genes. This must also have been why Aunt Ruth and Uncle Bill watched me and fussed over me. They wanted me not to die or kill myself like Jim, and so I didn't tell them about my sore back.

It was at Uncle Bill's that I was thrown from a horse and fractured my spine. This was later, of course, when I was about fourteen. This was just another of the disasters that seemed to attend them, that when they took care of their beloved niece for a whole summer month, she cracked her spine. So I didn't tell them how my back hurt. Perversely enough I didn't tell my parents either, but lay in pain for weeks, creeping slowly around, strong agony shooting up my backbone. But I never let any of them know.

A high-strung man, Uncle Bill eventually got an ulcer from worrying about what women would wear and buy. In those days ulcers were more serious, and he was advised to change his life. They bought a motel in Ukiah, California—a funny choice for a fastidious and worldly couple—and settled into the new life, which he managed to infuse with stress all the same, anxiously looking up and down the highway at sundown for people to pull in, following the maids around to check their work, obsessively attacking a weed here, wiping a dust particle there.

Perhaps my uncle Bill died in his heart when his cat Butch died—or, I should say, when they had Butch put down. Perhaps, for that matter, that decision had killed Aunt Ruth too, for she suddenly died, right after they sold the motel and moved to Southern California to be near me. Such a bad decision was like them—I could not then have said why, but it was characteristic of their combination of despair and optimism.

Perhaps a lot of people were like them, who were formed during the thirties and the Depression and going out west and so on, so the habit of changing jobs and places just hung on, driven by their determination to Make It, whatever It was, always warring with their genteel poverty, hardworkingness, and gaiety. Having focused on a dream of retiring to Long Beach, California, believing it un-likely that Butch, an old ginger cat, would be allowed in an apart-ment there, they had him put down, and it was just like them, and it probably killed them, or so I think now.

Once installed in Pacific Palisades, my uncle fell into a de-pression, and in revenge or despair, my aunt Ruth had a heart attack and died. She had confided a premonition about it, about trouble carrying groceries up her stairs, a painful feeling in her chest. Of course I didn't pay attention; I had a new baby, and another three kids at home, with the oldest just turned six. My brother, a medical student, was at the hospital when she was brought in. "Don't tell Bill until tomorrow," whispered my dying aunt Ruth, solicitous of Uncle Bill's sleep. She was younger than I am now.

Through them I first encountered both racism and anti-Semitism, though they were not racists or anti-Semites. When he was told about Aunt Ruth's death, my stricken uncle had said through his tears, "Call Herbie," Mr. Solomon from New York. Mr. Solomon asked me to arrange for flowers from him in Cali-fornia, and when I ordered them in his name, Forest Lawn kept insisting that I must want them sent to the Jewish part of the cemetery, Mount Sinai, as if it were impossible that someone with a name like Solomon could have been a friend of someone being buried in the non-Jewish part. This was a worldview I had not come into contact with before.

The racist incident was even dangerous: I went to visit Uncle Bill, now a broken and lonely man living in a motel in Ukiah, and took my children and the babysitter, Ev, who lived with us and was African American. While I talked to Uncle Bill, they went to swim in the motel pool. I've put this in a novel, but it really happened. Things like this did happen in America, I knew, but they had never happened in front of me: the motel owner screaming at Ev, "Get your black ass out of here," the children cowering and crying. And when I rushed to intervene, the fat, red-faced old man brandished a shovel at me.

I started to call the police, I was going to accuse him of attempted murder—but Ev and Uncle Bill both stopped me. She said it would do no good and he didn't want to be made to move. In the end we did nothing, nothing at all, except to remember this ugly thing and to understand things we hadn't understood before.

It's horrible to realize that I don't remember whether I put my uncle in the madhouse before or after this incident. Did he become depressed just after my aunt's death or after he had gone back to Ukiah? Did I drive up to Ukiah to pick him up, or was he visiting us when the decision had to be made? There was no one else to sign the papers, I was the only one. Consigning him to electroshock or whatever they thought they should do in the madhouse in Yountville: "Are you sure you're okay with this, Uncle Bill?" It was the public madhouse because, after all, he had no money, and neither did I.

What did he say, what words of acceptance, resignation, indifference, when I asked him whether it was all right to put him in a loony bin? I remember the horror of the locks on the doors made my ears hum. He said, "I guess so, Din."

Not that the doctors weren't polite, careful, optimistic that they could help. Not that the place was dirty—it was clean—but all the same, strange howls emanated from the other rooms, and people looked at us with wild, tormented eyes, and there was the pervasive smell of medicine and pee.

I can quickly summarize the traumas in my own life: my little dog Marco was run over when I was off swanning around Europe, something I often still think about with a stab of guilty sorrow. My divorce in the sixties I counted as an upbeat event to think about when I needed to cheer myself up. I haven't ever really been sick. But there was one other thing.

Sometimes I imagine that I must have experienced some childhood trauma so deep I have forgotten it; otherwise, how can I have had such a bland and uneventful early life? In my imagination, a recognition of some terrible event would unfold slowly in the course of me being psychoanalyzed. Perhaps this is why I've never cared to be psychoanalyzed. But I do remember one other thing, and that I still remember it suggests it was a major event in my life, at the age of five or six.

We made May baskets at school to take home to our mothers, and so I took mine home, hung it on the doorknob, rang the bell, and ran away. However, my mother didn't come to the door! How could that be? I tried another time, ran away, hid, and no one came. By the third or fourth try, I was in tears, frantic with an astonished sense of abandonment. Now my mother heard me and rushed to console me. She'd been in the basement or somewhere. I was home a bit early. That's it, my most traumatic memory. How could I look at an African child?

How could I not apologize for the shallowness of my emotional life, how take seriously my own tears? What a setback for a writer to have no more than this to complain of. Even in my most unhappy days since then, maybe before I realized I could divorce, sobbing in the bathroom to conceal my unhappiness from my children, part of me knew I didn't know what suffering was; I'd seen the dark shadow, that day at the movies.

Divorce

It only came to me slowly that I didn't have to be married. It was an unhappy time, that marriage, though I have repressed the details of why this was so. Now it seems to me that marriage is a happy state—now that I've been married happily for forty-five years. Then, for a dozen years, it was unpleasantness—arguments, he struck me once. In the main, our unhappiness was more existential, boiling down to not liking each other, something lots of couples endure more gracefully than I. I told myself it would be better for the children to see life represented by a happy mother, not a sad one sobbing in the bathroom.

Outwardly we were a normal couple, the husband rising in his medical hierarchy, the mom working on her novel, the children in the best elementary school. I signed up for graduate classes at UCLA, and though I didn't tell myself they were a path to self-sufficiency, that must have been the reason. If you take enough classes, you can get a Ph.D. And a job to support yourself and your four kids.

Then too, I was drawn to the life of the mind, of literature, poetry, and thoughts, and I was happiest in the UCLA library reading Spenser and Chaucer, and the Victorian novels Miss Garst had taught me to prefer. Literature was like Moline, or best of all the Europe I imagined—rich, ample, layered, patinated. Yet here I was in California; the library was the next best escape. The best escape was, at last, abroad.

London

So I was happy, happy, happy to be divorced, and take my kids and my little alimony, for those were the days of alimony, and my Wood- row Wilson Grant, and some money from the American Associa- tion of University Women, and every other cent I could cadge up, and go to England for scholarly work like a grown-up—not by sea, alas, but on one of those charter flights people flew in the six- ties, that stopped in Gander, Newfoundland, on the way, and you

Simon, Darcy, Amanda, and Kevin posing with me just before we left for London

tottered around to stretch your legs under a midnight sun, and then in the dawn arrived in the land of your dreams, England, land of Chaucer and Shakespeare and Henry VIII and Winston Churchill—land of all that had formed and instructed us, so I thought, heart pounding with joy and awe. At last, at last, I was in a foreign land, land of our backbone, our literature—our fascination with their kings and queens by far exceeding a native Englishman's.

The taxi driver from Heathrow cheated us, of course—I verified later in *Europe on 5 Dollars a Day* that it shouldn't have cost six pounds to get from the airport bus to Hampstead, where I'd reserved for us at a bed-and-breakfast I'd found in the same guide. But I was so thrilled to be in England—land of Big Ben, and the Tower, and Angus Wilson—that it didn't matter; I'd dreamed of this my whole life, and each detail of Londonness— the wrong-sided traffic, the iconic black cabs, the drab brick façades, thrilled me from my first footfall on English soil.

And the children had slept well on the plane from California and weren't as fussy as they might have been; they were thrilled too, to be in a fat London taxi, all of us, and all our luggage, and the cabbie with his Eliza Doolittle accent and plaid cap. He must have felt guilty about his swindle, for he said, "'Ere, luv, let's get you some fish and chips." We were starving. That would be another two pounds, but never mind—I figured out the prices of things soon enough.

A pound was worth more then, more than five dollars each, and we had very few of them, dollars or pounds. Other hurdles were even higher—finding a furnished house to rent, finding schools. Friends in America had suggested Hampstead—congenial community, slightly arty, good schools, direct Underground to the

British Museum, where I was planning to work. I had all my credentials ready to present.

I was writing a book about a Victorian heroine, a forlorn lady who had left her husband. How strange that one can have a relationship, a friendship even, with historical personages, and they become real. I had felt close to her because I too had left my husband, and here I was in England, with my four children, and Vicky, a morose au pair girl who had come with us from California, living in a rented house in Golders Green under false pretenses.

How naïve I'd been to imagine you could just find a house in England and move in, as you could in California. I soon learned too that a woman alone with four little kids and a surly teenage helper was not a welcome client to an English estate agent. Usually I got no further than the receptionist with her fluty voice: "I'm sorry, madame, we have nothing like that for you."

That time in London was the first in my life—it remains the only time—I've told a full-scale lie, a con, devised a fraudulent scheme to mislead, for I soon enough discovered, guided by their questions and seeing where they led, that I had to imply that I was there to settle in, enroll the children, and stock the cupboards before my busy doctor husband turned up. There was the lie—he was never coming; I hoped never to see him again.

I could confidently fill in the financial queries—$750, without mentioning it was alimony; and another $650 from renting out my house in Los Angeles. I had found a reliable tenant—Lola someone, an anthropologist. Margaret Mead herself had called on her behalf. We could live on $1,400, the four children, Vicky, and me.

"My husband isn't good with domestic arrangements—he leaves that sort of thing to me," I told the estate agent, Mr. Wickle. He understood, it sounded plausible to him—he himself, a husband too, wouldn't want to have to look for schools, in his tight English-tailored double-vent pinstripe, his vowels slightly off to my American ear, trained on Olivier movies and John Gielgud.

Well, in the end he would regret trusting me. I paid the deposit, and the first and last months of the lease, on a nice house in Golders Green, on Princes Park Avenue, just near enough to Hampstead that the children could go to the Hampstead Garden Suburb School, which came well recommended. Simon was in kindergarten; Amanda and Darcy, in second and third grade; and Kevin, in fourth grade. Vicky would take them the short walk to school, across the busy Finchley Road, and I would go off to the British Museum on the Underground. It was a nice four-bedroom house with a big kitchen and the ugly English cheap furniture a rented house would have there. It was perfect.

In the British Museum, I planned to work on the life of Mary Ellen Peacock Meredith, the daughter of Shelley's friend, the writer Thomas Love Peacock. Mary Ellen Meredith's is another story, one that I wrote and published a few years after all this, called *Lesser Lives* (1972). Before marrying George Meredith, Mary Ellen had been married to Edward Nicolls, a young naval officer who was drowned, and while I was working on Mary Ellen's story, I came under the spell of her first father-in-law, General Sir Edward "Fighting" Nicolls, a British seagoing soldier—a Royal Marine, a man who had, it seemed fruitlessly, struggled to save the world from tyrants, slavers, American insurgents, colonial brutes of every sort and the enemies of England generally, been wounded for every good deed, and never lost heart. Nor was he able to affect the course of history in the slightest. What an emblem of human stamina and principle, I thought. And of human futility too. He came to fascinate me; he became one of my captains.

As a child, like many nearsighted, puny little kids, I developed crushes on people in the books I read, and in landlocked Illinois, it was inevitable, or at least ironic, that I would be most drawn to seagoing tales and heroes, as I have mentioned. I devoured whatever accounts I could find by and about sea captains, and gentlemen deckhands, and pirates, imagining it was me before the mast, and it was a taste I've never outgrown. Only a few years ago I read every one of Patrick O'Brian's tales about Captain Jack Aubrey, some of them twice; I reread Conrad and Melville and Marryat at intervals, and also the lives of Nelson, of Scott and Shackleton and their foolhardy explorations, even of Captain Bligh . . . and Fighting Nicolls, who was born (like O'Brian's hero Jack Aubrey) in 1779, the same year Anne Cossitt Perkins was born, far away on the border with Canada.

One thing that I loved about Fighting Nicolls was his resolute optimism in the face of every sort of defeat and setback. For instance, he had tried to free American slaves in 1812, fifty years before they were freed for good. He issued an emancipation proclamation, and posted it all around New Orleans, and in Florida—but then was chased off by Andrew Jackson before he could implement his virtuous plan. Noble failure was pretty much his usual fate.

The English are on such intimate and friendly terms with their ancestors, even the most raffish or criminal ones, and one of

Nicolls's descendants, Eleanor de Montmorency, had promptly re-
plied to my inquiries about the Nicolls family. Lady de Montmorency and I sat in the tearoom of the old Civil Service Stores off
Trafalgar Square, talking of her forebear. She had apologized for
looking rather battered and skinned, with two black eyes and nose
empurpled. She was not really hurt, she said, she just "tookatoss,"
leaving me to wonder if she meant that she had fallen from her
horse, as unlikely as this seemed for a woman in her eighties. It
was so, though. "I was really not badly hurt—being rather like my
tough old great-grandfather, I think!" The way Fighting Nicolls
was an inspiration to me, along with the courageous Mrs. Meredith, now Lady de Montmorency—redoubtable old survivor, of
unfailing charm—was also inspiring, getting up and right back on
her horse.

She was born in 1888, but her great-grandfather was born in
1779 in Coleraine, in Northern Ireland, to Jonathan Nicolls and
a lady recorded only as the daughter of a Rev. Bushe Cuppage.
He went into the Royal Marines when he was sixteen. A Royal
Marine wouldn't have an easy life, he must have known, but a
young Irishman did not have as many choices as an Englishman
did. Where he went to school is not recorded, but because sixteen was relatively late to go to sea, it's safe to think he had already endured his terms at school, if not enjoyed them.

"I fear his entrance into the service did not improve his spelling," said Lady de Montmorency, reviewing one of his anxious
imploring letters to higher authorities, to some good end, always
in vain. Besides freeing American slaves, he tried to eradicate
slaving ships, and he hoped to dissuade the Maoris from canni-
balism and cure his own men from the demon rum.

I had tried to imagine how the young Edward must have felt
in the beginning, putting out to sea, though my own personal
experience of ocean voyages had still been limited to my imag-
inings during childhood hours spent in the *Unc*, our rowboat in
St. Ignace, tightly tethered to the dock, gazing out into the
whitecaps of the oceanlike Straits of Mackinac, reading *Two
Years Before the Mast* and *Captain Blood*. At least, I knew what it
was like to gaze on a whitecapped body of water with no opposite shore visible, the sense of limitless sea, and the suddenness
with which that water can grow black and tormented, the waves
can mount to house height in minutes. But I had never slept in a
small boat, and could only imagine the close quarters where Edward had to hang his hammock among snorers and bullies, and
I could imagine the bilgy smell.

Already at sixteen, he was an older boy. Sometimes in those
days, boys put out to sea, if they were sent to the navy, at nine
or ten, little boys, meant to serve and be educated by the captain. Perhaps you could be older in the marines, where you were
never destined to command at sea, though you had to fight
there, and on land as well, you were both fish and fowl. As a
marine you were conveyed across the seas by naval commanders
who might or might not be smart, who might refuse or accept
your good ideas—Edward's brain burned with ideas to conquer,
to defeat the enemies of England, and to distinguish himself. He
wanted to make a name, which he soon did, in his twenties:
"Fighting Nicolls" he would be called, after the affair of the *Al-
bion*, though it didn't go too well for him really. Though he was
admired for his valor in capturing the French ship at age twenty-
four, he didn't get the credit he should have, and was wounded to

boot. He was my hero and inspiration throughout some dark winter days in London, or one of them, for Mrs. Meredith was inspiring too. I was tracking her descendants via the wills in Somerset House.

The children were thriving in England. Off they went to school each day in their little gray shirts, neckties, knee socks, and navy skirts or short pants. We drank big cups of tea in the morning, with lots of milk, and sometimes we had bacon, and always had porridge. We felt very English, though they reported being called in their school "the Yanks." Simon, aged five, had a disappointment at his kindergarten when another child was chosen instead of him to play Jesus in the Christmas pageant. It came out that this was because Davey, a thalidomide child, could take off his legs, and thereby fit into the manger.

The kids were profiting enormously, after their lefty American experimental grade school, from the rigor at Hampstead Garden Suburb, which taught them things their progressive American school didn't believe in—cursive and the multiplication tables. Their voices developed British intonations, and a new vocabulary. I became "Mummie." "Mind the lift," they would say. They didn't dread the winter closing in, though the snow, after a snowstorm rare for England, panicked and delighted these little Californians who had never seen deep drifts and branches sagging low under great wedding cakes of powder. We bought duffel coats and mittens from Selfridges. It was a revel of McVities chocolate-coated wholemeal biscuits and Cadbury's too-sweet, horrible sweets.

Only Vicky was lonesome and restive. She turned out not to be good at chatting up people in pubs or otherwise meeting

people her age, and I didn't know anyone for her to meet. My own friends had young children the ages of mine, no one suitable for her; my friends were young writers starting out themselves, whose names I'd been given by my publisher. Now they are all Dames and Sirs—those who are still alive. I think of poor Jim Farrell, drowned in Ireland while fishing.

Vicky would be a beauty eventually, but then had a cross, disappointed expression, baby fat, the odd zit. I wrote anxiously to her mother, who had no suggestions beyond hoping for the best, and I grew paranoid seeing Vicky mailing letters, sure she was detailing cruelties on my part, and her misery, and her wish to go home. She couldn't go home; my life depended on Vicky.

So I was maybe the least happy person in our little household, living in terror about the fourteen hundred dollars and whether it would last and how to stretch it, and that we'd be discovered in our lie. Once, I had seen Mr. Wickle, the estate agent, standing in front of our house, looking thoughtful, and my fears shivered and boiled through sleepless nights. Mr. Wickle had checked up on us another time, once coming in to casually ask how "Dr. Johnson" was enjoying London and when had he got here. "Fine, a while ago, loves it," I said. I thought of buying some conspicuously masculine object, say, a pipe, to leave around in case he stopped in again. What if he asked the children about their dad?

Then too, I was repining for the married man I was in love with, in California, something I couldn't discuss with anyone. This didn't stop me, though, from smoking a joint from time to time with a former American boyfriend, himself in London, living with a fragile Irish novelist whose crises were so numerous he too had need to escape his ménage. We commiserated, were

both like sailors at sea, far from land and loved ones, in sinking boats.

During the day, sometimes I took the children out of school to do Anglophile things like standing in the throng lining a street to see the queen go by in her coach to open Parliament. We went to the flea market at dawn in Bermondsey and bought copper pans I still use, splendid pans from some great kitchen, bearing the monograms of the stately homes they came from.

In the Reading Room, I was completely happy, lost in history, especially in the manuscript room, thrilled that a person such as I was allowed to handle a letter written by Napoleon or Joseph Conrad or Mrs. Gaskell. Documents and manuscripts were bound together hodgepodge in fat miscellaneous volumes, and you never knew what you'd find by turning the leaves. When you asked for, say, the logs of Captain Mudge, you might also get poems in Shelley's handwriting, Sarah Bernhardt letters, meet someone unknown, a new friend from the past; and I would read through the whole wad of treasures at once, the afternoon slipping by in a haze of happy reverie. In the manuscript room, an austere, warm space down the hall from the venerable and glorious round Reading Room, all blue and gold, where no pens were allowed, and the chairs were just uncomfortable enough to recall the reader to a sense of privilege and awe.

I was looking for letters from Meredith or Peacock, to do with Mary Ellen, but sneaking time to read about Fighting Nicolls or the French Revolution instead, or Fabian tracts. Napoleon had a pretty, artistic hand, and a precise mathematical ability, calculations in ink now faded to brown. He could calculate the volume of water in a ditch, or the number of men needed to dig it. The most famous letters of the British Museum were upstairs in cases to be read by everyone ("It seems a pity, but I do not think I can write more" [Scott], or "Oh miserable wretched Emma / Oh glorious & happy Nelson" [Lady Hamilton]). But many more were under my hand in the manuscript room.

In the library, I was happy, but my stomach would begin to crawl with panic and inadequacy as soon as I got on the Northern line home. My trustful children would be drinking their after-school tea and doing their homework, overseen by the glowering Vicky, none of them knowing my secret economies or how close we were to having no money at all. So far I'd found nothing about Mary Ellen to speak of. I sent off letters to the various heirs I'd tracked down in wills filed at Somerset House, and waited for answers that rarely came. It was dark now by four in the afternoon, and the kids went to school mornings and came home in darkness.

I couldn't have been doing this at all if it weren't for Vicky, yet I worried my freedom couldn't last, she was too unhappy.

"I tried it," she'd say when I suggested getting out at night, going to pubs and movies. "What assholes. You can't talk to anyone. They hate Americans, and they're all too plastered to make any sense."

Church groups? Adult education? She had a certain scornful way of looking at me when I suggested these desperate and probably futile ways of meeting people. What did I know? I'd never been a woman on the loose, was married too young, and now was impeded from adventures by having fallen in love with the man in California. He called us in London once or twice a week, but sometimes I hadn't got home yet and the kids answered, or Vicky did, and would just tell him I wasn't there. So I seldom talked to him, and didn't have that much to say except that I missed him. I didn't know if he cared about Napoleon's being good at math.

"Half the time I can't understand a word they say," Vicky said of the people in the pubs. "I thought we all spoke English here. Ha."

41

Emancipation Proclamation

My aim was ostensibly Mrs. Meredith, but I continued to track Fighting Nicolls too, and have watched for him over the years since. I mention him for the pleasure of it, because of his tutelary role in my psyche, holding out against all odds. I had some luck with Mrs. Meredith too. I'd tracked down and written to a certain Mrs. Whiting, in Croydon, who had inherited the estate of a Mr. Wallis, son of Henry Wallis, the minor Pre-Raphaelite painter who was Mrs. Meredith's lover. Though the odds were slim that Mrs. Whiting would know anything about these departed Victorians, it was at least a lead. Mrs. Meredith was also an inspiration, defying convention to run off with a lover. I tried not to think about her fate—early death, forgotten and alone, as in a Victorian novel.

Parallels between my life and Fighting Nicolls's impressed me with superstitious encouragement. He had found himself in American waters off Louisiana in 1814. He was then thirty-four, my very age, had been in the marines for eighteen years, was a major, and already an experienced commander, there to lead British troops against Andrew Jackson. It's certain he'd spent some time ashore in England, he'd married somewhere along the line, perhaps had children by then, like me. He must have had news of Wellington's victory at Waterloo, though Europe was far, and news traveled slowly.

In New Orleans he tried to get the cooperation of a local warlord, Jean Lafitte, the pirate. I was thrilled to read this—I had loved Lafitte too when I was a child, the dashing young man of good family turned buccaneer—the very ideal of a pirate, as played by, say, Tyrone Power. Edward sent two envoys to visit Lafitte in his lair and deliver a letter:

Sir,

I have arrived in the Floridas for the purpose of annoying the only enemy Great Britain has in the world [America]. As France and England are now friends, I call on you with your Brave followers to enter into the Service of Great Britain in which you shall have the ranks of Captain. Lands will be given you all in proportion to your respective ranks on a Peace taking place, and I invite you on the following terms. Your property shall be guaranteed to you and protected, in return for which I ask you to cease all hostilities against Spain or the Allies of Great Britain—your ships and your person protected, to be placed under the orders of the commanding officer on this station untill the commander in chiefs pleasure be known. . . .

I herewith enclose you a copy of my Proclamation to the inhabitants of Louisiana which will I trust point out to you the government; you may be a useful assistant to me. . . .

Lafitte was a Creole, that is, French and Spanish, raised in the Caribbean, without deep loyalties or antipathies, except for his dislike of England, which pretty much doomed Edward's appeal from the start, though Lafitte appeared to think over his offer. Lafitte enjoyed easy social relations with Americans, and with the best social set in New Orleans, and went to the best parties.

Pensacola was a poor place, hot, bug-infested, with a pitiful population of scruffy Indians and slaves, and Edward had quickly decided to make the best of them, poor fellows; of course they

would see it was in their best interest to cast their lot with England. His proclamation addresses all "the free coloured inhabitants of Louisiana," explaining his plans to liberate them from "a
faithless imbecile government. . . .

> There will be paid the same bounty in money and lands,
> now received by the white soldiers of the United States, viz.
> one hundred and twenty-four dollars in money, and one
> hundred and sixty acres of land. . . . You will not, by being
> associated with white men in the same corps, be exposed to
> improper comparisons or unjust sarcasm.

Fighting Nicolls was and remains an inspiration to me when times
are dark.

42

Defeat

Snug and happy though we were throughout the London winter, a blow awaited us, not from Mr. Winkle, as I expected, but from Lola the anthropologist, who, despite her lease, notified me she planned to move out of my house in Los Angeles in May, that is, in a few weeks. She had some good excuse, though I didn't believe her. Without the rent, we couldn't pay our rent in London, and we therefore couldn't stay; all was over. I told Mr. Winkle, and though I expected he would be glad to be rid of us, he was remorselessly vindictive about lease breaking, and threatened to sue if we left before he had found someone else to rent the house.

At first it appeared he had found a tenant to replace us, but not before I'd lain awake nights pondering our options—a cheaper place, which was probably impossible, but for which, anyhow, I lacked the will and organizational powers to hunt, and then to subject the kids and Vicky to. I imagined a Dickensian debtors' prison, Mr. Winkle at our heels, academic blackballs, squatters in our L.A. house when Lola left it vacant. Fighting Nicolls would not have been daunted, but I was daunted. Then the relief of Mr. Winkle's announcement, then the horror when his new tenants did not have promising references, and we had already bought our tickets home.

And I'd by no means been done with Fighting Nicolls and never would be, but was obliged to say good-bye to Lady de Montmorency.

"I'm afraid I left my woolly at Derry and Tom's," she said on the telephone. "I'll be going there to pick it up; perhaps we could have tea there. Not that I have much more to tell you. You know he fought against the Americans. But when my parents went to Sea‑ ford (in Sussex) they decided to get rid of so many papers, et cet‑ era, as they could, as they did not want to have too big quarters. So one of my sisters' husbands burned masses of papers, records, let‑ ters (and even sermons!) for them, and cleared up everything so that they only had a small amount of furniture and personal things to have with them. There were, I think, certainly, some diaries there belonging to my grandfather—'your' Edward's brother— who died in India during the mutiny—all most interesting—and there were also diaries kept by General Sir E.'s wife, while he was often at sea, or governing one of his islands. But all these must have been cleared out with other papers. . . ."

For so it is all too often, the historian is cheated by exasper‑ ated descendants who have too little room in their closets, and the attic is a thing of the past.

I had better luck with Mrs. Meredith. In Croydon, under the bed in the box room, where I'd been given permission to rum‑ mage, a wad of tiny letters, two by four inches, in a tiny hand, hidden in a paint box: Mary Ellen Meredith to Henry Wallis, her lover, alone, penniless, trying to put on a brave face.

43

Yellow Morgan

Before I had to leave London I did one totally American thing to cheer myself up. Would I have gone to an auto show if I did not also have the normal American obsession with cars? Looking back, I can't explain this fit of madness except as a deep need for life to take an interesting and cheerful, bright yellow turn. I took the children to the Earls Court Motor Show, and there mort, gaged my future to buy a chrome yellow Morgan sports car.

I can't reproduce the state of mind that took me there, but I told myself it was out of necessity—I'd need a car once we got back to L.A. I'd sold my 1956 Beetle, the kind that didn't have a gas gauge. (Once I forgot, and we ran out of gas. My husband at the time raised his hand to strike me. It was the end of our mar, riage anyway.) And now I was in England, at Earls Court, think, ing again about wheels.

Earls Court, an exposition space sometimes dedicated to dog shows or garden equipment, had become a dreamland museum of unattainable Rolls,Royces and heart,stopping Jaguars. Once there, my fascination bloomed into desire, its object being a Morgan drophead roadster, an export model unspoken,for be, cause of its left,hand drive.

The price was sixteen hundred pounds, and it stood like a sculpture on a dais, with a long line of people waiting their turn to sit in it, hold the steering wheel, and dream. We (my four little children and I) waited in line and sat in it. The children made engine noises, *vroom, vroom,* and took turns steering.

I knew at once that I had to have it, that this was my car. But since I had no money and no British bank account, how could that be done? I pleaded to be the buyer over the palpable misgivings of Mr. Morgan himself, a little man in a sweater vest, on whom I exerted my utmost wiles to convey plausibility and solvency, and was eventually permitted to sign the bill of sale. My children spun around me in delirious excitement. He would reserve the car for me: I would have the money on Monday morning. He hoped so. It was unusual in Britain then, apparently, for a young woman, with a flock of children at her heels, to walk in someplace and buy a car.

In truth, I had already tied up a sum on a sensible Volkswagen squareback to be picked up later in Wolfsburg. (I had mostly owned German cars; maybe it's like sexual preference—you tend to go on as you started.) So I had no more money, but I had friends, or so I thought until I began making frantic phone calls to America. No one—not my parents, my married lover, or my better-financed friends—would lend me the money to buy a silly English sports car I didn't need.

"English cars are terrible, think of Jaguars, always in the shop."

And no one failed to point out that I was a single mother of four young children, who couldn't possibly even all fit into a two-seater, even if I let them ride in such a death trap. Telegrams, imploring phone calls, desperate promises, nothing availed.

Finally, my loyal younger brother in Los Angeles relented. Perhaps he was the only one who understood the intangible allure of certain cars. He, after all, owned a black Citroën Pallas sedan with gangster-black one-way windows, and a mysterious way of rising on its air suspension like an inflating blimp—a car so glamorous that film directors used to slip their cards under the wipers. My brother was also a co-owner, with me, of our family's 1964 red Impala convertible, which he has stored in his garage to this day because we can't bear to part with it. Like the VW, the Morgan was shipped to California. (Eventually I ended up selling the VW at a profit, and the Morgan too.)

That sports car was the culmination of a lifelong interest in cars but also, I think, the beginning of an aversion to driving. It was the world's most uncomfortable ride. Added to the other discomforts of convertibles (their exhilarating features aside) were the discomforts of its suspension—its frame, after all, was made of ash wood. Did it have shock absorbers? Perhaps not. After my sixty-mile commute each day, bones rattled, spine contorted, I could barely walk. And I need not speak of the danger. Worse was the police officers' attraction to this yellow apparition; they were always stopping me to inspect the equipment and challenge the size of the headlights or the height of the bumper. I never got a ticket, but was always getting pulled over, even, one day, twice.

The Morgan was a powerful symbol, and I had succumbed to it in the face of the sheer impracticality, even foolhardiness, of owning it. That we all dream of ourselves in cars is well known; that they express our fantasies is a commonplace. Looking back, I can see it was a car of protest; I was protesting my life. I had some wish to see myself as not weighted down, not a Beetle person (as I am now), not a member of the carpool and station wagon set, but free and frivolous. What it symbolized to the police officers I can only imagine. Perhaps they were drawn like bees to its buttercup color, or like male animals to the estruslike call of its muffler, or perhaps they were infuriated by the scofflaw attitude implied by its outrageous deviation from common sense.

I don't always know what people mean by cars being their embodied images—I missed the meaning of Saabs, for example. I don't know why the elderly Italians in my neighborhood have to have Chryslers. But as Americans we probably do have to own our dream car, and even display it, be seen in it at least once. We can tell our life stories as a sequence of cars.

I went back to America with my yellow Morgan, and England had changed me completely. V. S. Pritchett says in his autobiography, of his move to France as a young man, "I became a foreigner. For myself, that is what a writer is—a man living on the other side of a frontier." I had crossed one frontier when I went to California, but never so far as when I went to England. There I got a taste for foreignness, and eventually, like Pritchett, went to live in France.

Chagrin

Which is how, years later, John and I found ourselves at the house party in Provence. And there is another logic to the story: the *Chicago Tribune* appeared on our doorstep each morning throughout my childhood with headlines pertaining to War or Roosevelt in large black letters, along with columns my mother consulted for child-rearing advice. Apart from the newspaper, in Moline we were not much more in touch with the outside world than were our forebears, and my longings for it were literary rather than based on an actual sense that it was real and accessible. I followed the war almost as an abstraction, but I did follow it, and have been interested in warfare ever since, along with sea voyages.

So when we visited the generals in Saint-Pantaléon, I was interested that the talk was of the Second World War, and of the upcoming preparations to commemorate the sixtieth anniversary of the Normandy invasion, where General Rolfe had been an important figure, though only a young captain at the time. The faint regretful tone of the others, who were slightly younger, reminded how small are the windows of opportunity for military glory. If by a trick of birthday you have missed this important battle, that decisive war, then you have missed it, and have to settle for cold Korea or for quartermastering in North Carolina.

Generals have lots of interesting stories, as you might imagine. It had surprised me that they were religious, both involved with Mennonite and Catholic and Huguenot history. Religion and ancestors—the twin institutions humanity has fastened on to put its faith in. Either seemed odd for military men, especially since they themselves were used to being the repositories of other people's faith. William Baum talked a little about how it was to know that not only all the men but all their mothers and fathers looked to you, the commanding officer, not for absolute protection against death but for assurance that death would be met arbitrarily, by bad luck, not by worldly mistakes. He was talking not about his own career—he was far too modest and gracious—he was talking in the abstract about how the support for fighting in Vietnam had eroded at home. People had died from mistakes, malice, bad morale, and friendly fire.

We commented on General Baum's pacifism. "Professional soldiers are the last ones in favor of wars," he said. We noted the ostentatious modesty of his calling himself a humble "soldier," not even "officer."

As we got up to go to bed, Sally Rolfe said, "My turn for dinner tomorrow, I hope someone can drive me to the market good and early."

"I'll drive you," John offered. "Willard and I have a rematch tomorrow morning. The court's right near the market square. I noticed it today."

"Oh, you and Diane will still be here? Oh, good," she said.

To this, Simone gave such an odd glance, first at me, then at Sally, I feared that we had taken her by surprise. Hadn't we said we'd be staying one day, that is, tomorrow? Perhaps she had counted this little leftover part of the day today and had supposed we would be leaving in the morning. I worried that Simone had someone else coming, and needed our beds. But wouldn't she have told me?

When I had a chance, I asked her. "No, no one, it's wonderful

that you're here," she said, firmly and warmly, so I put it out of my
mind. But at the market, looking at the vast circus of gladioli and
lilies, the clouds of gypsophila in the flower stalls, she all at once said,
"I'd be nuts if you hadn't come, and we still have ten days to go."

I took this to be a continuation of the former conversation.
"Difficult guests?"

"I've known them for years, but I never had to live with
them. Sally and Lynne, especially. It's exhausting. Their competi-
tion. Each bouquet of a greater perfection, each flower more rare,
each dinner more ambitious. We are already exhausted. They
have known each other for decades and they still want to win." We
talked then of the hard culture of the corporate wife, for it was
surely the same for military wives: being watched by the higher-
ups who have the power to impede or advance your husband; being accountable to the husband therefore ("I think you may have
had a bit too much last night, dear"; "Isn't that skirt a little long/
short?"); having to be better than the other wives—forget sister-
hood, forget working, forget eccentricity.

No wonder they have a reputation for drink, military wives.
You couldn't blame them. I thought of all those rumors about
Mamie Eisenhower. But Sally, Lynne, Cynthia, and Simone did
not drink too much. They did not do anything too much, judging
from the perfection of their figures, the decorous restraint of their
beautifully graying, undyed hair (I wasn't so sure about Lynne's).

We had decided to stay until at least tomorrow afternoon to
allow for more tennis. John was happy, having fallen in love with
Willard Lee, the perfect tennis opponent, tireless, avid, and a shade
better than John, or at least in better practice. After a cold indoor
winter in Paris, punctuated by infrequent long metro trips to the
Bois de Boulogne for tennis sessions merely forty-five minutes long,

the prospect of a sunny morning on the courts tomorrow over-
came him. I offered to be responsible for the lunch.

"Certainly not, darlin', it's all arranged," Cynthia Baum had
assured me. "We've got our KP rotation all worked out, we're delighted." I liked her best, she was the warmest and most natural.

"The men should take Lynne along to play tennis. She'd
never say so, but I know she'd like to, she's always the champion
on any base we were ever at," Cynthia had said handsomely so
that Lynne could hear; Lynne smiled slightly and said she would
love to play. I, knowing how John hates to play mixed doubles,
did not volunteer him.

I didn't understand them. These were the successful women,
wives of successful husbands, ones who from the starting gate
had finished the race. Yet something was strained and off.

In the morning, Simone and I wandered in the flower market.
I had once overheard someone, another American tourist, looking
at a flower stand, say, "You know it's a good civilization by the way
they always have fresh flowers, everyone, every day." Of course
this wasn't literally true, not everyone every day—but it was almost true, flowers were integrated into the way of life, florists'
shops every block or so in Paris, and here—this must be sort of a
wholesale depot—an unimaginable quantity, a whole botanical
garden of vivid glads and spiky red things I didn't know the name
of, late irises, zinnias in their millions, lacy festoons of gypsophila,
blossoms smug knowing themselves, as the flower grower knew
himself, to be essential to human happiness.

I had been thinking about happiness lately, because of getting a
letter from a more or less always unhappy friend, just before
coming away, and thus having it in my mind to send a card to her

from somewhere along the way here, but also wondering, as I always did with her, if it were somehow wrong to intrude one's own happiness (meaning, natural placidity plus good luck so far in not having very much to worry about) on someone who really did, objectively, have terrible things go wrong for her—autistic child, her sister's suicide, that whining husband. And it's easier to feel happy when you are on vacation, and not in America, where you would be worrying about guns, politics, and crime. I was sure they had politics and crime in France too, but somehow those were their politics, their crime, and I meantime had the sight of their beautiful azure cornflowers—all the flowers have different names, though, in French than what we would call them. These were *bleuets* or *barbeaux*. I was so happy being in Europe, the way lots of Americans are. Why is that? We must ask ourselves.

Simone and I went straight from the courtyard into the kitchen with our arms full of flowers—*bleuets*—and she went to the pantry for a vase, so that for a moment I was alone to hear voices in the living room. Angry voices, an animated argument, the Baums and the Rolfes, and Lynne Lee. The higher voices of the women, and their extra passion, told above the deeper, perhaps more pacific, male voices. You couldn't help but listen, and, as the old saw has it, the eavesdropper hears ill of herself. And now Simone had come in again and so she could hear ill of herself too. Their bitter quarrel was about her, and us.

"Ah don't care, we're spendin' ten thousand dollars a month here, and for Simone to bring in extra people and they don't put in a nickel, and this is the second damn time she's done it, that's takin' advantage." Cynthia Baum's Southern voice.

"I am certainly not going to bring up money with Stuart," said General Rolfe. "In his state of health."

"You're right in a way, in principle, of course, Cinny, they should pay their share. But we only have ten more days, it'll just go more smoothly if you don't say anything," agreed General Baum.

"You could say something to him," said Sally Rolfe. "He seems all right. The husband."

"Next time, if there is a next time, we'll agree on the battle plan straight beforehand. We should have done that. We should always do that. We can take some of the blame for not doin' that."

"Simone thinks we're these captive moneybags, she can bring in her friends to freeload. It just floors me!" Cynthia Baum said again.

"If you won't say anything, I will, I believe in things out in the open. I just feel if we have all this anger, it will just spoil things in the future. It's much better to get it out. But I resent how I always have to do the damn dirty work" (from Sally Rolfe).

Should they reproach us directly or let it slide? Should they insist later that Simone pay for us? (For it was true, invited guests, we hadn't paid our share of two nights' rent. Hadn't thought of it.) And so the argument went, without them resolving a course of action, but just teasing their indignation into new shapes. Simone, frozen, listening for a long moment, now plunked the vase into the sink with a loud noise (perhaps cracking it), saying to me, "*Alors*, it is the lunch that smells so *délicieux*." And just then John came in from our room, showered, by the look of his wet hair.

"Something smells good," he said, looking hopefully at the pot and without asking taking a beer from the fridge, a beer his inviolable habit after tennis.

"But we can't stay," I cried, the miserable consciousness of what they had been saying only now making its implications felt. "We have to go now, before lunch."

"What are you talking about?"

"Shhh," moaned Simone, "she can tell you outside," and she shoved us out by the pantry door. Outside, I explained: the generals hated us being there, we hadn't paid for our share of the rent, they were angry at Simone for inviting her friends on their dime. We couldn't stay. It was hard for John, hearing our version at second hand, to feel the same shock and chagrin as I did, but at last he agreed we should probably leave.

"Unless that would somehow reveal that we'd overheard, which would make it embarrassing for the Wards," he pointed out.

"No, you must stay, *mon dieu*," said Simone, grimly. "This is between me and them. *Incroyable!* I don't want Stuart to know." Her face was aflame. I kept insisting we go—how could we sit there, after all, eating their food? I was embarrassed beyond bearing it; all of life's embarrassments came rushing back: The spot on the back of my dress at graduation. The time I threw up in the potted palm in the lobby of the Muehlebach Hotel in Kansas City. The time I backed into the policeman. And it was then that the episode of the *fundoshis* came back to me, when the general's elegant daughter saw my father dressed like Mahatma Gandhi. Where do these things lurk until they come rushing back? Their cruel edges dulled only slightly.

Because of dancing class at the Rock Island Arsenal, I had known a succession of playmates whose dads were generals or sometimes colonels, uniformly glamorous fathers, in their spangles, and, I thought then, incalculably grander than my own father, who did not wear a uniform. On the contrary, he had once been spied inadvertently in his underwear by me and my friends as he blurted out onto the landing of the stairs to say something to my mother. What made it terrible for me was that my father wore as underwear an eccentric garment known as a *fundoshi*.

Through the democratic institution of the clothesline, in those days before dryers, my father's *fundoshis* must have been known to all in the neighborhood, but not to the colonel's daughter, Helen W., who was with me on the stairs. A *fundoshi* is a rectangle of cotton cloth worn like a loincloth, and had been recommended to my father and several of his friends on the grounds of comfort and masculine health by a golfing companion who had discovered them in India. Gandhi wore them, I believe. But I still remember—perhaps I imagined—Helen's look of supercilious shock.

Now, despite our embarrassment, we were soon installed at the lunch table, changed, brushed, our car packed, trying to ignore what we had heard. *Soupe de lotte au safran.* With it we drank the red we'd brought.

"Very good, these light reds with fish," said General Baum in tones of heartiest goodwill.

After lunch, as we made ready to depart, John had a chance to raise a delicate point with the generals, off to one side, under the portico. "This has been so nice, Bill, but you have to let us chip in for our time here," he began.

"My dear fellow, out of the question," said General Baum. "What an idea! It's been absolutely delightful." The wives crowded in.

"Any friend of Simone's . . ." Cynthia agreed. "We just adored meeting you."

"We should pay you for getting old Willard out there on the courts, out of our hair for hours at a time," said Lynne, smiling.

"We'll get you back when we come to California," said General Rolfe. "Look for us one of these days." You could not but admire the perfection of their demeanor, their affable farewells, their genial reminders of future meetings and instant rapport.

"All that delightful wine, thank you endlessly," cried Simone, eyes blazing, thrusting herself into the midst of the amiable good-byes as if to cut off an unendurable spectacle. Later, in the car, I calculated that our share would have been thirty-two dollars. But of course we ought to have thought of it. Simone never would tell us what the final reckoning had been, when they did their accounts at the end of their stay.

As the days went by, embarrassment at our obtuseness was not what stayed on my mind; it was the idea of soldiers' mothers, confiding their sons to generals of whom they do not know the souls. I can imagine soldiers' mothers better than I can imagine soldiers; but I can imagine being a soldier too, in a hot concrete bunker somewhere, trusting in the greatness of my general, so I hoped— that distant, august figure in charge of my life, not knowing that in life they could seem otherwise.

Epilogue

A few years ago, I wrote an essay about the weddings of my chil‹dren. My husband, John, and I have seven children between us, and they are all married, some of them twice. Most of them have married people from other lands and races. This gives us an assortment of daughters‹in‹law and sons‹in‹law more varied, perhaps, than in most American families, and an even more ex‹otic array of cograndparents. The tone of my original essay was one of light appreciation, but I now see that it might also have contained a tiny note of self‹congratulation for our good charac‹ter in welcoming and tolerating this disparate bunch of relatives, self‹congratulation poorly merited, for we are, I sense, more de‹tached than some sorts of family, more timid of interference, for all our goodwill. I fear our perfect toleration contains a tinge of lazy laissez‹faire. ·

Briefly, in order of chronological age, our oldest son was mar‹ried to a Hawaiian but is now married to an Australian. Our second son is married to a woman from Ireland, and our third son, who was married to an American (raised, however, in Ger‹many), is now married to a Chinese wife from north of Beijing. Then comes Darcy, whose husband is exotic to us only by being a Republican, then Elizabeth, who is divorced from her WASP doctor husband, Bri—the only one of our sons‹in‹law to resemble my husband; our third daughter is married to a French architect, and our youngest son to a flowerlike Japanese. These last two families live in France and Japan, respectively, and Doug and

Bernadette have lived about half their married life in Ireland, but otherwise they are all in America.

We choose not to think that their marriage choices, of people as unlike us as can be, are meant to be rejections of us, a possibility some mean-spirited friends have pointed out. Our theory is that our children have married these people of various nationalities and have adopted international habits because we traveled with them when they were children, took sabbaticals abroad. And, most important, that this is the American family of the future, races and nationalities and languages blended into a kind of improved alloy, requiring toleration and humor.

Meantime we, John and I, spent more and more time in France. Simone's implicit question stayed with me: what was I doing in France? Everyone knows you can't really leave wherever you started, a message reiterated in all the literature of the world. What had I been doing in California, for that matter? Why had I so burned to leave Moline? Wondering about that, I went back to see it—the occasion was a high school reunion. It had been more than a half century since I'd been there. Everyone should go to a high school reunion at least once. I took two of my children and my brother's youngest daughter along with me so that they, California kids, could have some idea of family history, roots, America.

We drove down from Chicago in a rented car, and tooled around the streets we remembered. We looked at our house, and the grave of Charles Dickens's boy Frank, and the Congregational church, where serendipitously the organist was practicing Bach, and sunshine flooded in through the stained-glass window, affirming my impression of the peace and beauty of our childhood religious experiences. It was autumn, and the leaves were changing. The town was much more beautiful than I remembered, much more lush than California; and the sight of the wide, great, brown river stirred me unexpectedly. At Black Hawk State Park, unchanged in most respects, the scalp that used to hang from the ridge pole of the exhibition building had been taken away, no doubt to give it a respectful burial, and dioramas of Native American life were new, but I think some of the moccasins and beads were the same.

The reunion dinner was at the country club at the Rock Island Arsenal, so I visited the armory museum there beforehand. Had I ever been taken to it as a child? It was unfamiliar, and so much more interesting than I could have imagined, with cannonballs and matériel produced there in the somber Civil War buildings. I had remembered the rows of Confederate graves, prisoners who died, mostly of typhus. An air of historic gravity belied the trendier emplacements now installed along the Iowa shore, with its retro riverboat casino and the art museum designed by the famous English architect David Chipperfield. Downtown Moline was not much changed. The soda fountain Lagomarcino's was still there, but coffee is espresso now. I had become someone else, and was not really in touch with Moline, but I could see that it was now more in touch with the world. As for Kevin, Darcy, and niece Katy, I can't say what their impressions really were, but they were good-natured travelers and cheerfully bore the breaded shrimp and the hectoring of Fox News in every roadside diner we stopped in, as cultural tourists in a heartland they'd never imagined.

So I suppose this is really a travel book, beginning with the desire of a small midwestern child for adventure, preferably at sea, before the mast. But unlike another book of mine, *Natural Opium*, which tells about going to new places with my husband, John, this one travels back in time, with the excuse that looking

at the Midwest of long-departed people and even my own childhood could remind of things people talk about as being missing
in America today, and help remedy our apparent inability to
learn from other cultures that might be doing things that if we
did them too would restore the charm and goodness of our own
society—trains, for example, and nice long vacations. Mom-and-
pop restaurants!

We can all confess to a disappointment or two in life—I would
have really loved to be an opera singer, and of course, like anyone,
I'd have preferred to be prettier, smarter, and more talented, and
to be leading a life of adventure and moral courage. Many of my
friends have personal histories of considerable interest and even
universal significance—my friend the writer Millicent Dillon
worked at Oak Ridge, Tennessee, in 1945, for instance. Another
friend, the novelist Carolyn See, has a moving story to tell about
the role of drugs and alcohol in her family—as in many American families. Every soldier has a major life-and-death account. But
my own life is lacking in drama, and the worst thing I can remember happening in Moline in childhood is when a neighbor boy
killed some newborn rabbits with a spade. Why did he do that? I
never heard if he grew up to be a serial killer, though I know his
brother grew up and bought an island.

Nostalgia can add up to a hopeful reminder that, having always been told ours is the best society, we could look at ourselves
more squarely and recognize that in places where we aren't the
best, we could improve. For my part, I know I always fall down on
self-improvement resolutions, but I hope tomorrow I will be better, and in saying so I sound to myself just like great-great-
great-grandmother Anne Perkins at the end of the eighteenth
century, as if nothing changes at all.

ACKNOWLEDGMENTS

How can I thank enough the many people who have helped with this book, either by agreeing to read it and advise (my husband, John Murray, and patient friends John Beebe, Mary Blume, Helen Brann, Robert Gottlieb, and Alison Lurie) or by checking my recollections against theirs: my brother, Mike Lain; my friends from grade school Alyce Keagle Ritti, Faith Carlson McWilliams, and Laura Pelletier; my Moline lunch friends Gay Fahrner and Stephanie Peek—and to the memory of the late William Theophilus Brown? I also thank the Cossitt family association, especially its officers, Campbell Cossitt and Richard Frey, for material on the earliest arrivals; the Vercler family in Chenoa; Lucy Gray, who photographed the paintings of Eleazer and Catharine; Peter Galassi; Marilyn Drew and Alison Owings, for help with quilts; friends and colleagues at the Sewanee Writers' Conference for listening to passages several years running; and of course my agent, Lynn Nesbit; my editor, Carolyn Carlson; Ramona Demme; and the rest of the team at Viking, who have been wonderful.